RENEWED PRIMARY FRAMEWORK

100 MATHS

HOMEWORK

ACTIVITIES

Ann Montague-Smith, Claire Tuthill
and Richard Cooper

YEAR 4

Credits

Authors
Ann Montague-Smith, Claire Tuthill
and Richard Cooper

Development Editor
Nicola Morgan

Editor
Ruth Burns

Assistant Editor
Margaret Eaton

Illustrations
Andy Keylock (Beehive Illustrations)

Series Designer
Helen Taylor

Designer
Macmillan Publishing Solutions

Mixed Sources
Product group from well-managed
forests and other controlled sources
www.fsc.org   Cert no. TT-COC-002769
© 1996 Forest Stewardship Council

Text © Ann Montague-Smith,
Claire Tuthill and Richard Cooper
© 2009 Scholastic Ltd

Designed using Adobe InDesign

Published by Scholastic Ltd
Villiers House
Clarendon Avenue
Leamington Spa
Warwickshire CV32 5PR

www.scholastic.co.uk

Printed by Bell and Bain Ltd, Glasgow

1 2 3 4 5 6 7 8 9   9 0 1 2 3 4 5 6 7 8

British Library Cataloguing-in-Publication Data
A catalogue record for this book is available from the British Library.

ISBN 978-1407-10219-1

The rights of Ann Montague-Smith, Claire Tuthill and Richard Cooper to
be identified as the authors of this work have been asserted by them in
accordance with the Copyright, Designs and Patents Act 1988.

Extracts from the Primary National Strategy's *Primary Framework for
Mathematics* (2006) www.standards.dfes.gov.uk/primaryframework © Crown
copyright. Reproduced under the terms of the Click Use Licence.

Contents

Homework

Homework: Counting, partitioning and calculating

Homework: Securing number facts, understanding shape

Homework: Handling data and measures

Homework: Calculating, measuring and understanding shape

Homework: Securing number facts, relationships and calculating

Puzzles and problems

Answers

Introduction

About the series

100 Maths Homework Activities offers a complete solution to your planning and resourcing for maths homework activities. There are six books in the series, one for each year group from Year 1 to Year 6.

Each *100 Maths Homework Activities* book contains 72 homework activities, which cover the Renewed Framework objectives, and 36 puzzles and problems, which focus on the Using and applying objectives.

About the homework activities

Each homework activity is presented as a photocopiable page, with some supporting notes for parents and carers provided underneath the activity.

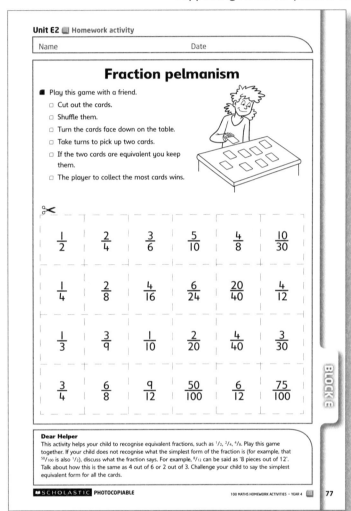

Teachers' notes relating to the activities appear in grid format at the beginning of each block's activities. When exactly the homework is set and followed up is left to your professional judgement.

Across the *100 Maths Homework Activities* series, the homework activities cover a range of homework types. Some of the activities are for sharing. These encourage the child to discuss the homework task with a parent or carer, and may, for example, involve the home context, or a game to be played with the carer. Other activities involve investigations or problem-solving tasks. Again, the parent or carer is encouraged to participate in the activity, offering support to the child, and discussing the activity and its outcomes with the child.

Using the homework activities

Each homework page includes a 'Helper note', which explains the aim of the homework and how the adult can support their child if he or she cannot get started. It is recommended that some form of homework diary be used alongside these activities, through which to establish an effective home-school dialogue about the children's enjoyment and understanding of the homework. A homework diary page is provided on page 6 of this book.

Teachers' notes

The teachers' notes appear in a grid format at the start of each block's homework activities. Each grid contains the following information:

- the Framework unit
- the homework activity's title
- a brief description of the format and content of the activity, which will help you to decide which homework activity to choose
- the Renewed Framework learning objective/s
- a 'Managing the homework' section which provides two types of help – 'before' and 'after'. The 'before' notes provide suggestions for ways to introduce and explain the homework before the children take it home. These notes might include a brief oral activity to undertake as preparation for the homework. The 'after' notes provide suggestions for how to manage the review of the homework when the children return with it to school. Suggestions include discussing strategies used for solving a problem, comparing solutions, and playing a game as a class.

◤ SCHOLASTIC

About the puzzles and problems

The puzzles and problems (pages 90-107) provide coverage of the Using and applying mathematics objectives and can be used very flexibly to provide children with a comprehensive range of fun maths tasks to take home. The grid displayed on page 89 shows which puzzles and problems cover each of the Using and applying objectives.

Puzzles and problems

5 Concert tickets

Tickets to the Locomotives concert cost £8 each.

Bruce has £63.

How many tickets can he buy?

6 Lucky numbers

Jade says the difference between her two lucky numbers under 100 is 17.

What could Jude's lucky numbers be?

Give three suggestions.

1 _____

2 _____

3 _____

BINGO

92   100 MATHS HOMEWORK ACTIVITIES · YEAR 4   PHOTOCOPIABLE ■SCHOLASTIC

The puzzles and problems are based on work that the children will be covering during the year and should test their skills at that level. Some of the questions may be solved quickly, others will require more thought. Either way, children should be encouraged to try a variety of different approaches to solving problems and to look for clues and patterns in maths. It is essential for them to read the question carefully (sometimes more than once) to understand exactly what they are being asked to do. A few of the puzzles and problems will require an everyday household item or the help of a family member. Most should be readily solved by a child working on their own.

Remind the children that if a problem or puzzle is proving too difficult or frustrating, they could leave it and come back to it later with a refreshed mind!

Developing a homework policy

The homework activities have been written with the DCSF 'Homework guidelines' in mind. These can be located in detail on the Standards website **www.standards.dfes.gov. uk/homework/goodpractice** The guidelines are a good starting point for planning an effective homework policy. Effective home-school partnerships are also vital in ensuring a successful homework policy.

Encouraging home-school links

An effective working partnership between teachers and parents and carers makes a positive impact upon children's attainment in mathematics. The homework activities in this book are part of that partnership. Parents and carers are given guidance on what the homework is about, and on how to be involved with the activity. There are suggestions for helping the children who are struggling with a particular concept, such as ways of counting on or back mentally, and extension ideas for children who would benefit from slightly more advanced work.

The homework that is set across the curriculum areas for Year 4 should amount to a total of about one and a half hours per week. The homework diary page, which can be sent home with the homework activity with opportunities for a response from the parents/carers, can be found on page 6 of this book.

Using the activities with *100 Maths Framework Lessons Year 4*

The activities covered in this book fit the planning within the book *100 Maths Framework Lessons Year 4* (also published by Scholastic Ltd). As teachers plan their work on a week-by-week basis, so the homework activities can be chosen to fit the appropriate unit of work.

Name of activity & date sent home	Child's comments	Helper's comments	Teacher's comments
	Did you like this activity? Draw a face. a lot a little not much / How much did you learn? Draw a face. a lot a little not much		

Counting, partitioning and calculating

Activity name	Learning objectives	Managing the homework
A1		
Times-tables practice Write table facts for numbers in the 2-, 3-, 4-, 5- and 10-times tables.	Derive and recall multiplication facts up to 10 × 10, the corresponding division facts and multiples of numbers to 10 up to the tenth multiple	**Before:** Recite the tables quickly together. Remind the children that if they are not sure about a number, this is one way to check which table it appears in. **After:** Discuss how the children worked out which numbers did not belong in the tables. They may point out that both numbers are odd. (Both are prime.)
'Less than' snap Play a game of Snap to practise using the 'less than' symbol (<).	State inequalities using the symbol < (for example, −1 < +1)	**Before:** Demonstrate the game to the children. **After:** Ask if the children found any strategies to win.
Timed challenge Answer mentally (or with rough jottings) a series of addition and subtraction questions, using a range of strategies.	Add or subtract mentally pairs of two-digit whole numbers (for example, 47 + 58, 91 − 35)	**Before:** Discuss methods that can be used. **After:** Ask individual children to tell you how long they took and go through any methods that helped them to solve each question.
Colour by numbers Use colour-coding to begin to learn the multiplication facts for the 6-, 7-, 8- and 9-times tables.	Derive and recall multiplication facts up to 10 × 10, the corresponding division facts and multiples of numbers to 10 up to the tenth multiple	**Before:** Talk through the method for colour-coding. It may be an idea to ask the children to make a list of all the numbers in the times table. **After:** Talk through the questions at the end of the worksheet.
A2		
Adding Work through addition questions, writing the calculations vertically as well as horizontally.	Refine and use efficient written methods to add two-digit and three-digit whole numbers	**Before:** Remind the children how to set out a vertical addition question, and to add the most significant digits first. **After:** Work through the examples together. Invite children from each ability group to show the others by writing on the board how they worked out an answer.
Multiplication and division practice Answer four questions involving multiplication and division, to be discussed with a helper.	Develop and use written methods to record, support and explain multiplication and division of two-digit numbers by a one-digit number	**Before:** Review multiplication and division written methods. **After:** Invite a child from each ability group to explain, writing on the board, how they found the solutions.
Counting on Practise using the counting-on method to solve some subtraction questions.	Refine and use efficient written methods to subtract two-digit and three-digit whole numbers	**Before:** Review using the counting-on method for subtraction. **After:** Invite children from each group to explain, using the board, how they worked out the answers to one question.
Column skills Work out some column additions and then check answers, using another written method or talking through a mental method.	Refine and use efficient written methods to add two-digit and three-digit whole numbers	**Before:** Discuss how to set out and work out addition totals. Recap checking techniques. **After:** Go through individual examples.

Counting, partitioning and calculating

Activity name	Learning objectives	Managing the homework
A3		
Shopping trip Look at an illustration showing a range of different objects and select as many items as possible that make exactly £2.50.	Solve one-step and two-step problems involving numbers; choose and carry out appropriate calculations	**Before:** Discuss the list of rules. **After:** Compare results. Who was able to buy the most items? Which items did they buy?
Beat the clock Helper reads out some addition and subtraction questions for child to answer mentally or with rough jottings.	Add or subtract mentally pairs of two-digit whole numbers (for example, 47 + 58, 91 − 35)	**Before:** Discuss methods that children can use to help them answer the questions. **After:** Choose a few children to tell you how long it took them to answer the questions and which they found the most difficult.
Subtracting columns Work out some column subtractions and then check answers, using another written method or talking through a mental method.	Refine and use efficient written methods to subtract two-digit and three-digit whole numbers	**Before:** Discuss methods that children can use to help them answer the questions. **After:** With the class, go through individual subtractions on the worksheet.
The crossing-out challenge Find and cross out numbers on a grid that satisfy different rules.	Solve one-step and two-step problems involving numbers; choose and carry out appropriate calculations	**Before:** Discuss an example and the vocabulary used. **After:** Go though individual examples on the worksheet. Ask the children to provide some of their own number sentences.

SCHOLASTIC

Name   Date

Times-tables practice

◖ Look at the numbers in the grid.

◖ Choose a number and write its times-table fact.
Work against the clock.

  ☐ Be careful! There are 12 numbers, but two of them are
not in the 2-, 3-, 4-, 5- or 10-times tables.

◖ Write the two numbers that are not in the 2-, 3-, 4-,
5- or 10-times tables in the boxes at the bottom of the
sheet.

15	18	24
36	35	23
90	19	20
45	27	32

× =	× =
× =	× =
× =	× =
× =	× =
× =	× =

◖ The two numbers that do not fit in the tables are: ☐ and ☐ .

◖ Time taken: _____

Dear Helper

Your child has been learning their 2-, 3-, 4-, 5- and 10-times tables. This activity will help your child
to recall some of the facts. Please time how long it takes them to do this activity. If your child does not
remember some of the facts, ask them to say the tables through and search for the fact. Remind them,
though, that two of the numbers in the grid do not belong to the tables. Challenge your child to see if
they can find more than one fact for any of the numbers.

BLOCK A

Name   Date

'Less than' snap

- ◼ This is a game for two or more players.
- ◼ Prepare some cards displaying the numbers in the grid shown here.
- ◼ Instructions:

  ☐ Write the numbers on card or paper. Cut them out and shuffle the cards.

  ☐ Deal the cards equally between the players.

1	2	3	4	5	6
7	8	9	21	22	23
24	25	26	27	28	29
41	42	43	44	54	67
89	121	134	155	143	117

  ☐ The first player puts two cards into the boxes below to make a correct number statement. For example, 2 < 11 (two is less than eleven).

  ☐ Players then take turns to place cards into the correct boxes, on top of the cards that are already there.

  ☐ If a player puts a card into an incorrect box, then she or he must pick up the pile.

  ☐ The winner is the first player to get rid of all their cards.

- ◼ When you have played the game once, repeat – but this time try to do it a little faster.

Dear Helper

This activity will reinforce the idea of 'greater than' and 'less than'. If your child is finding it difficult to place the cards on the correct pile, it may be helpful to draw crocodile teeth onto the inside edges of the 'less than' sign and say: *The crocodile always eats the larger number.* When your child places a card on a pile, encourage them to say, for example, *1 is less than* 7, or *7 is greater than 1*. For more of a challenge, prepare some cards with three-digit numbers, such as 543, 435 or 354.

Name   Date

Timed challenge

◖ Work out these additions and subtractions in your head, using the methods that you have learned this week.

◖ Think:

☐ Can you make pairs of numbers that could help you?

☐ Can you round the number up to the nearest 10 to help you?

☐ Ask your helper to read out the following questions, and to time how long it takes you to answer the set of ten questions.

1.   23   +   17   =   _____

2.   80   –   12   =   _____

3.   29   +   11   =   _____

4.   30   –   18   =   _____

5.   47   –   18   =   _____

6.   12   +   78   =   _____

7.   100   –   34   =   _____

8.   49   +   11   =   _____

9.   17   +   4   =   _____

10.   29   –   8   =   _____

◖ How many did you get right?   _____

◖ How long did it take you?   _____

◖ If any were incorrect, try again using the written methods you were shown in class. Show your workings out on the back of this sheet.

Dear Helper
This activity will help your child to develop methods for adding and subtracting mentally. If your child is stuck, ask them to look at the last digits. With 23 + 17, for example, you can add together the 3 and the 7 to make 10, and then add 30. For subtraction, it may help to subtract the nearest multiple of 10, and then add on the difference. With 47 – 18, for example, work out 47 – 20, understand that you have subtracted 2 too many, and add that on at the end. It would be helpful, at the end of the timed activity, for you to go through the questions and ask: *How did you work that one out?* As a challenge you could ask your child to think of another way to get the same answer.

Name	Date

Colour by numbers

■ Using colouring pencils, follow the instructions below.

☐ Colour in all the numbers in the 6-times table red.

☐ Colour in all the numbers in the 7-times table blue.

☐ Colour in all the numbers in the 8-times table green.

☐ Colour in all the numbers in the 9-times table yellow.

☐ If the number is not in the 6-, 7-, 8- or 9-times table then leave it uncoloured.

6	7	8	9	10
16	17	45	19	20
26	27	28	29	30
35	37	38	39	40
14	21	12	49	50
2	57	58	59	60
66	32	64	69	70

■ Now answer these questions:

1. What is the sum of all the numbers coloured red? _____

2. What is the difference between the largest number coloured green and the

smallest number coloured green? _____

3. How many more blue numbers are there than yellow? _____

Dear Helper
This activity will help your child revise their 6-, 7-, 8- and 9-times tables. It may be helpful to ask your child to write down these tables in lists on another piece of paper before they start (1 × 7 = 7, 2 × 7 = 14 and so on). As a challenge you could ask your child to look at the numbers not yet coloured in and ask: *Which numbers are even? Which times table would they be in?* (The 2-times table.) *If we coloured in the even numbers, is there a times table that would include most of the remaining numbers?*

Name	Date

Adding

- Do these sums two ways.
  - ☐ Work horizontally. Show your workings.
  - ☐ Write the sum vertically. Show your workings.
- Share your work with a helper.

$37 + 63 = 90 + 10 = 100$

$$
\begin{array}{r}
37 \\
+\ 63 \\
\hline
90 \\
+\ 10 \\
\hline
100 \\
\hline
\end{array}
$$

1. $65 + 45 =$

2. $83 + 89 =$

3. $123 + 45 =$

4. $246 + 78 =$

Dear Helper

Your child has been taught a method for working out addition. Listen to your child explain how they have worked out the answer. Try not to be tempted to teach your child a 'quicker' way as this method is part of the Primary National Strategy. If your child struggles with these questions, suggest that they work horizontally only. They can add the hundreds, then the tens, then the units, and finally total all of these. (You probably learned to add starting with the units.) Challenge your child with an example such as 357 + 246 (500 + 90 + 13 = 603).

Name   Date

Multiplication and division practice

◾ Use the way you have been shown at school to do these problems.

◾ Explain to your helper what you are doing.

$56 \times 7 =$	$83 \times 5 =$
$35 \div 5 =$	$72 \div 6 =$

Dear Helper
Your child has been doing multiplication and division problems at school. They have been learning ways to do them that you might not have seen before. Ask your child to explain how they have found the answers. Try not to show them a method that you think might be quicker because the method that your child is using is the recommended method of the Primary National Strategy. Ask your child to explain, for each question, what they are doing and why, and how they have found the answer.

Name	Date

Counting on

▰ Practise subtracting numbers using the counting-on method.

▰ Explain to your helper how you worked out each one.

▰ Here is an example to remind you:

$$
\begin{array}{r}
345 \\
- 76 \\
\hline
\end{array}
$$
4 to make 80
20 to make 100
200 to make 300
40 to make 340
5 to make 345
269

1. 456 – 68 =

4. 991 – 76 =

2. 631 – 87 =

5. 436 – 77 =

3. 357 – 89 =

6. 841 – 75 =

Dear Helper

Your child has learned a new method of subtraction that involves 'counting on'. Ask your child to explain how this method works. If they find the method difficult, please do not teach an alternative one. The counting-on method is the one recommended by the Primary National Strategy, and is the one your child's school is teaching. If your child finds the questions on this page easy, challenge them to make and try to solve some four-digit minus three-digit questions, such as 1527 – 315.

Name	Date

Column skills

- Look at the pairs of numbers below.
- Using the space provided, set out and work out the total of the two numbers using the column method that you have been learning at school this week.

  ☐ An example has been included (right) to help you.

Example:

```
  1 4 5
+   8 9
  2 3 4
```

(check: 145 + 90 = 235, then subtract 1, so the total is 234)

Problems:

```
  1 6 9
+   9 1
```

```
  4 8 9
+   2 8
```

```
  2 3 3
+   1 8
```

```
  6 8 9
+   2 2 7
```

```
  4 5 5
+   3 9
```

```
  5 7 7
+   9 9
```

Dear Helper

This exercise will help reinforce the skills that your child has been learning this week at school about adding in columns. Please encourage your child to set out the questions carefully, ensuring that the units are beneath the units, tens beneath the tens and the hundreds beneath the hundreds. Ask your child to talk you through each stage of the calculation, especially any 'carrying over' to the next column. When your child is happy with their answer, encourage them to find an alternative method to check their answer, either by jotting down something different at the side or mentally by talking it through.

Name	Date

Shopping trip

◼ Look at the items available in Janni's local post office. She has £2.50 to spend.

◼ Work out what she could buy with her money. Stick to the following rules:

☐ She may only buy one of each item.

☐ She is aiming to buy as many items as possible.

☐ She is aiming to have no change left over at the end.

◼ Show your working out on the back of this sheet.

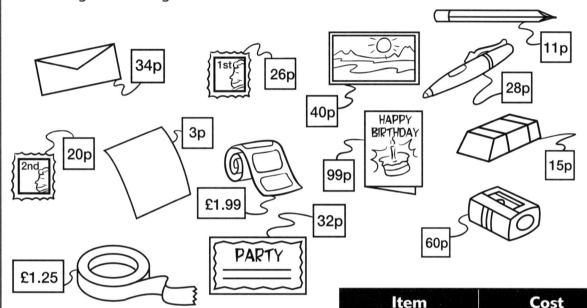

◼ Fill in the list (right) to show what she could buy and how much it would cost.

Item	Cost

1. Janni can buy _____ items.

2. They cost _____ altogether.

3. She will have _____ change from £2.50.

Dear Helper

Encourage your child to add the amounts together mentally and then check their answers at the end. If your child is not very confident they can make a list (ensure that the units are lined up correctly) and then add up the columns, or find pairs of numbers that they are able to add and then find the sums of these pairs. As an extra challenge you could ask your child to find a different combination of things to buy. Ask: *How much change would you have left? Can you still buy the same number of items? What if you were allowed to buy more than one of each item?*

Name   Date

Beat the clock

■ Ask your helper to read out the questions below and time how long it takes you to answer all 20 questions.

■ Work out the answers to the questions in your head, using the methods that you have learned this week.

■ Think:

   □ Can you make pairs of numbers that could help you?

   □ Can you round the number up to the nearest 10 to help you?

$23 - 19 =$ ☐ $23 - 21 =$ ☐ $36 - 28 =$ ☐

$87 - 19 =$ ☐ $45 + 21 =$ ☐ $70 - 38 =$ ☐

$45 + 19 =$ ☐ $26 - 21 =$ ☐ $37 + 28 =$ ☐

$26 - 19 =$ ☐ $36 - 21 =$ ☐ $56 - 8 =$ ☐

$36 - 29 =$ ☐ $70 - 31 =$ ☐ $25 + 57 =$ ☐

$37 + 29 =$ ☐ $87 - 28 =$ ☐ $29 + 13 =$ ☐

$27 + 9 =$ ☐ $46 + 18 =$ ☐

■ How many did you get right?   _____

   □ How long did it take you?   _____

■ Look at the questions again to see if you could have made things easier for yourself by using the methods you have been learning in class. Now repeat the test.

■ How many did you get right?   _____

   □ How long did it take you?   _____

Dear Helper

This activity will help your child to develop methods for adding and subtracting mentally. If your child is stuck, say, for example: *For 37 + 29, you can work out 37 + 30 and then take away 1.* For subtraction it may help to subtract the nearest multiple of 10 then add on the difference. For example, say: *For 36 – 28, work out 36 – 30. You have subtracted 2 too many so add that on at the end.* At the end of the timed activity go through the questions with your child and ask: *How did you work that one out?* As a challenge, your child could try to think of another mental method to use to answer the questions.

Name   Date

Subtracting columns

▪ Look at the pairs of numbers below.

▪ Using the space provided, set out and work out the answers to the subtraction questions below using the column method that you have been learning at school this week.

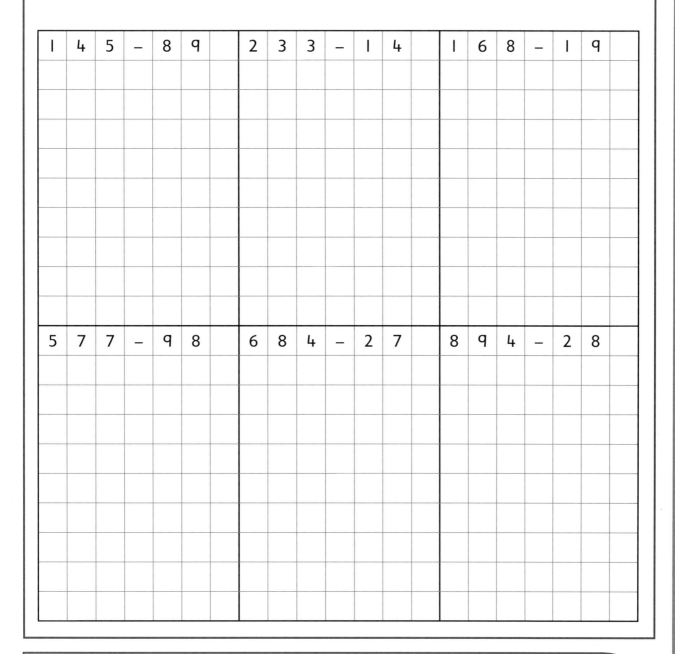

1	4	5	–	8	9
2	3	3	–	1	4
1	6	8	–	1	9

5	7	7	–	9	8
6	8	4	–	2	7
8	9	4	–	2	8

Dear Helper

This exercise will help reinforce the skills that your child has been learning this week at school about subtracting in columns. Please encourage your child to set out the questions carefully, ensuring that the units are beneath the units, tens beneath the tens and the hundreds beneath the hundreds. Ask your child to talk you through each stage of the calculation, especially any 'carrying over' to the next column. When your child is happy with their answer, encourage them to find an alternative method to check their answer, either by jotting something down at the side or mentally by talking it through.

BLOCK A

Name   Date

The crossing-out challenge

9	76	99	75
33	1	63	69
73	79	43	14
52	27	19	50

◢ Cross out the number that is the sum of 6, 1 and 2.   _____

◢ Cross out the two numbers that have the largest difference.   _____

◢ Cross out the two numbers that have the smallest difference.   _____

◢ Cross out three pairs of numbers between which the
difference is 10.   _____

◢ Cross out the number that is double 7.   _____

◢ Cross out the number that is half of 38.   _____

◢ Cross out the two numbers between which the difference
is 2.   _____

◢ Which number is left?   _____

Dear Helper
This activity will help your child to follow instructions and practise their calculation skills. Please make sure that your child follows the instructions in order and understands that once they have crossed out a number they cannot use that number again. Ask: *What does 'difference' mean?* (Take away.) *What does 'sum' mean?* (Add.) *What do we have to do when we double a number?* (Multiply by 2.) *How do we find half of a number?* (Divide by 2.) For a greater challenge, ask your child to make up another three sentences to describe a number in the grid.

Securing number facts, understanding shape

Activity name	Learning objectives	Managing the homework
B1		
All change! Count on and back in steps of the same size and record the sequence of numbers.	Identify and use patterns, relationships and properties of numbers	**Before:** Count together in sevens from 100 for ten steps. Then count back in sevens from 100. **After:** Invite children from each group to read out one of their sequences. The other children can quietly join in with the number sequence.
Missing signs Complete the missing signs in the number sentences.	Solve one-step and two-step problems involving numbers; choose and carry out appropriate calculations	**Before:** Write an example on the board such as 60 ? 5 = 12. Ask the children to explain what operator sign is missing, and why. **After:** Review the work together. Invite the children to explain how they solved the problems and to share questions they made up with the class.
Next in line A game for two players to practise number sequences.	Identify and use patterns, relationships and properties of numbers	**Before:** Run through the rules of the game and trial the game if time is available. **After:** Go through the number sequences involved – in particular the 'add 25' sequence – and ask: *Who won?*
Close enough? Choose the best method to approximate and check the answers to calculations.	Use knowledge of rounding, number operations and inverses to estimate and check calculations	**Before:** Discuss rounding up and down to the nearest multiple of 10. **After:** Compare answers. Did everyone agree?
Nutty nets Make a 3D shape from a net using squared paper.	Visualise 3D objects from 2D drawings; make nets of common solids	**Before:** Talk through the method of making a net of a cube; discuss faces and the use of flaps. Provide the children with squared paper for making their own nets. **After:** Compare and display the 3D shapes the children made.
Polyfolds Fold squares to form different polygons.	Draw polygons and classify them by identifying their properties	**Before:** Revise the names of polygons with various numbers of sides. Clarify the difference between irregular and regular shapes. **After:** Share the different solutions as a class.
B2		
Make it four! A 'doubles' game to be played with a helper.	Identify the doubles of two-digit numbers	**Before:** Give out the sheet and briefly explain the rules. **After:** Talk to the children about numbers they found hard to double.
Numbers against the clock A game for two players to practise number sequences.	Identify and use patterns, relationships and properties of numbers	**Before:** Run through the rules of the game. Play the game, adjusting the timings as necessary. **After:** Ask: *Who won? How far did you get with each sequence?*
Doubling game Cut out given number cards; shuffle, pick one and begin to double, taking turns. First person to go over 100 gets a point. Repeat.	Identify the doubles of two-digit numbers	**Before:** Ask the children to remind you of some strategies for doubling more tricky numbers that bridge the next 10. **After:** Ask the children to list, as a class or group, the doubles that they can Instantly recall.
Speed test for 4- and 8-times tables A times-table speed test for the 4- and 8-times tables.	Derive and recall multiplication facts up to 10 × 10, the corresponding division facts and multiples of numbers to 10 up to the tenth multiple	**Before:** Revise the 4-times table. Remind the children that the 8-times table is double the 4s. **After:** Compare times of successfully completed tests. Go through the 4- and 8-times tables with the class.

BLOCK B

BLOCK B

Activity name	Learning objectives	Managing the homework
Shape sifting Identify irregular 2D shapes and find lines of symmetry in 2D shapes.	Draw polygons and classify them by identifying their properties, including their line symmetry	**Before:** Remind the children what regular and irregular shapes are. **After:** Look at the examples of 2D shapes that children have drawn on the back of their sheets.
What makes the box? Investigate nets of cuboids.	Visualise 3D objects from 2D drawings; make nets of common solids	**Before:** Remind the children what the net of a shape is. **After:** Go through the answers with the class.
B3		
Card connect A 'follow me' card game to practise mental addition and subtraction.	Use knowledge of addition and subtraction facts and place value to derive sums and differences of pairs of multiples of 10	**Before:** Ask the children some two-digit addition and subtraction questions. Review with them how they found the answers. **After:** Use the activity again as part of a Starter. Encourage the children to complete it as quickly as they can.
Sums and products Find pairs of numbers that give a specific sum and product.	Investigate a statement involving numbers and test it with examples	**Before:** Ask the children to say which two numbers have the sum of 15 and the product of 50. (5 and 10.) Ask them to explain how they worked this out. **After:** Invite solutions from children from each ability group. Ask the children to explain how they solved the problems. Invite children to challenge the class with the extra problem they made up.
Times-tables investigation Investigate the statement: 'A number in the 10-times table must also be in the 2- and 5-times tables.'	Identify and use patterns, relationships and properties of numbers; investigate a statement involving numbers and test it with examples	**Before:** Talk through how you would like the children to record their results. **After:** Ask: *Who thinks that the statement is true? Why?*
Double dice A dice-doubling game to encourage the use of doubling as a strategy for adding.	Identify the doubles of two-digit numbers; use these to calculate doubles of multiples of 10 and 100	**Before:** Demonstrate how to generate the numbers, arrange and round them for Game 2. **After:** Ask questions such as: *What was the highest score reached in Game 1? What was the highest possible score in Game 2?*
What a thing to say! Decide whether the mathematical statements are true or false.	Report solutions to puzzles and problems, giving explanations and reasoning orally and in writing, using diagrams and symbols	**Before:** Remind the children of the mathematical language used in the activity. **After:** Go through the answers with the class. Discuss statements that the children have written.
Factors Identify factors of numbers up to 100.	Derive and recall multiplication facts up to 10 × 10, the corresponding division facts and multiples of numbers to 10 up to the tenth multiple	**Before:** Remind the children what a factor is. **After:** Go through an example question on the board.

Name	Date

All change!

◖ You will need a counter or coin.

◖ Begin with 56.

□ Toss a counter onto the number grid below.

□ Add the counter number to 56 again and again, at least five times. Write the sequence of numbers on the back of the sheet.

□ Make ten number sequences by adding.

□ Now, subtract the counter number from 100 five times.

□ Write the sequence of numbers on the back of the sheet.

□ Make ten number sequences by subtracting.

2	8	10	17
4	16	13	10
11	9	6	12
7	3	14	5

Dear Helper
This activity helps your child to count on and back in steps of the same size. If they find this difficult, say the start number together, then ask them to add on the counter number. Write down the answer, add again, and so on. For some numbers your child may spot a pattern. For example, add 9 gives 56, 65, 74 and so on – where the tens digit increases by 1 each time while the units digit decreases by 1. Challenge your child to write the sequence of numbers for each of the numbers in the grid.

Name   Date

Missing signs

- There are missing signs in these number sentences.
- Write in the signs so that each number sentence is true.

14 ☐ 28 = 42

100 ☐ 23 = 77

23 ☐ 6 = 138

102 ☐ 45 = 57

84 ☐ 6 = 14

Dear Helper
This activity helps your child to consider which number operation – addition, subtraction, multiplication or division – has been carried out to find the answer in these number sentences. Remind them that they must check that the sign works. If your child finds this difficult, talk through whether the answer is larger or smaller than the other numbers, and how much larger or smaller. (If it is much larger it is probably multiplication; much smaller is probably division.) Challenge your child to write some more questions like these to take back to school.

Name	Date

Next in line

● For this game you will need:

☐ scissors (to cut out the cards)

☐ a partner to play the game with.

● Instructions

☐ Cut out the cards. Shuffle and deal the cards equally between the two players.

☐ **Player 1** reads out the sequence on the first card carefully, and repeats it if asked. **Player 2** must then say the next number in the sequence and explain the rule.

☐ If Player 2 is correct the card is placed face down on the table and Player 2 now reads one of her/his cards to Player 1. If the answer is incorrect or partly incorrect it stays in Player 1's hand.

☐ The winner is the first player to guess all the sequences in their opponent's hand.

16, 18, 20, 22	100, 97, 94, 91
Answer: **24**	Answer: **88**
45, 54, 63, 72	34, 29, 24, 19
Answer: **81**	Answer: **14**
1, 12, 23, 34, 45	2, 27, 52, 77
Answer: **56**	Answer: **102**
14, 20, 26, 32, 38	80, 73, 66, 59, 52
Answer: **44**	Answer: **45**
53, 45, 37, 29,	45, 58, 71, 84, 97
Answer: **21**	Answer: **110**

BLOCK B

Dear Helper

This game will help your child practise number sequences. Make sure that your child does not look at the answers as they are being cut out. Play the first game slowly, repeating the sequences twice, then reshuffle the cards and play a little faster. Each time ask: *What is the difference between the numbers?* or *What has been added/subtracted?* For extra support, ask your child to write down the sequence as it is being read out. As an extra challenge, ask: *What would the next number in the sequence be?* or *What if we started with 99?*

Name   Date

Close enough?

■ Look at the following calculations and decide which is the best approximation.

■ Discuss your ideas with your helper.

1. Which of these do you think is the best approximation for 609 + 296?

600 + 97
600 + 300
700 + 300
700 + 200
610 + 290

_____

2. Which of these do you think is the best approximation for 19 × 7?

20 × 7
2 × 10 × 7
19 × 10
20 × 5

_____

3. Which of these do you think is the best approximation for 99 – 67?

100 – 70
100 – 60
100 – 67
99 – 70
99 – 60

_____

4. Which of these do you think is the best approximation for 349 – 99?

350 – 90
350 – 100

_____

5. Which of these do you think is the best approximation for 999 + 9?

990 + 10
990 + 9
1000 + 9
1000 + 10

_____

6. Which of these do you think is the best approximation for 49 × 5?

4 × 10 × 5
5 × 10 × 5

_____

Dear Helper

Approximating answers will help your child to know if an answer is correct or sensible without having to rely on a calculator. At school they have learned to round up or down to the nearest 10, so for example, 34 would be rounded down to 30, whereas 35 or 36 would be rounded up to 40. It would help to talk through the various options given before your child makes a decision, as there is sometimes more than one correct answer. As an extension you could challenge your child to work out the exact answers to these questions, which would allow you to compare the estimates with the answer.

Name	Date

Nutty nets

◀ Nets are the flat pattern for a 3D shape. For example, if you took a cereal packet from the cupboard and opened it flat, this would give you the net of a cuboid.

◀ You will need some squared paper.

◀ Look around your house for an empty packet. Ask permission to cut it open, lay it flat and look at the net.

◀ Take a few minutes to refold it back into a 3D shape and then dismantle it again to look at the net.

◀ Carefully draw the net of a 3D shape on the sheet of squared paper.

◀ Look at the faces and remember that the net may need flaps if you want to glue the 3D shape together.

◀ When you are sure, cut out your net and see if it folds into a 3D shape.

◀ Decorate your 3D shape if you have time.

Dear Helper
In school your child will have looked at various nets of a cube and how they fold to make the cube. Your child might have trouble visualising how the shape will fold up, so encourage them to look at the opposite faces and how the shape will look from the top, bottom, the sides, and so on. As an extra challenge, ask your child to sketch a different net that will fold to make the same shape.

Name   Date

Polyfolds

■ Cut out this square to help you with these puzzles.

■ By folding your square in different ways, see if you can create these different polygons.

☐ One fold to create an isosceles triangle.

☐ One fold to create an irregular pentagon.

☐ Two folds to create an irregular pentagon.

☐ Two folds to form an irregular hexagon.

☐ One fold to create another quadrilateral.

☐ Two folds to create an isosceles triangle.

☐ Three folds to create an irregular heptagon.

☐ Four folds to create a regular hexagon.

■ If you find a way of creating the polygon, mark the fold on the squares on the right with a dotted line so that you can discuss your findings with your teacher and the rest of the class.

■ What other polygons can you make by folding a square?

☐ Show any other results on the squares on the left.

Dear Helper

This activity reinforces the shape work that your child has been revising this week. Encourage your child to cut out and use the large square to help them investigate folding to create other polygons. An isosceles triangle has two sides of the same length and one of a different length; a pentagon has five sides; a hexagon has six sides; a quadrilateral has four sides; a heptagon has seven sides. A regular shape has all sides the same length and an irregular shape has sides of different lengths. As an extra challenge, encourage your child to write instructions similar to those given above to direct others to make the extra shapes that they have recorded.

Name	Date

Make it four!

◀ You will need counters or something similar to play this game. 1p and 5p coins are ideal but do give them back when you've finished!

◀ Take turns to point to a number in the top grid (for example, 41) and say, 'I can get double 41 by doubling 40 (pointing to that number in the bottom grid) and adding 2.'

◀ If your helper agrees that the answer is correct, you can cover the number in the top grid and the one in the bottom grid with your counters.

◀ The winner is the first person to cover four squares in the top grid. You can't re-use numbers that are covered in the bottom grid.

BLOCK B

29	38	41	59	61	9
22	57	53	39	82	19
81	99	21	18	49	91
43	89	11	31	92	51

100	80	30	120	160	100
120	60	40	180	60	120
40	80	80	20	180	100
20	180	60	100	20	40

Dear Helper

The process of doubling the numbers in the top grid is called using 'near doubles'. Each one is near a number that is easier to double, so we can do that and adjust the answer. An understanding of doubles is very important for children, as is an understanding of these near doubles. For example, double 42 is the same as 42 + 42, which is easier as double 40 then add 4. Alternatively, to add 38 + 38, double 40 then subtract 4. If your child is unsure about how to calculate near doubles, encourage them to use paper-and-pencil methods to help. Challenge your child to work mentally to find the near doubles.

Name   Date

Numbers against the clock

■ You will need:

☐ scissors (to cut out the cards)

☐ a stopwatch or clock

☐ a partner to play the game with.

Rule: add 2	Rule: add 3	Rule: subtract 3	Rule: add 10	Rule: add 9	Rule: take away 5
Rule: add 11	Rule: add 4	Rule: add 6	Rule: take away 7	Rule: minus 8	Rule: minus 4

■ Instructions

☐ Prepare the following numbers on separate pieces of card or paper, to be starting numbers:

   1   5   7   9   19   33   38   39   57   99   100

☐ Cut out the cards above and shuffle both sets so that you have two piles of cards, one with rules and one with starting numbers.

☐ **Player 1** picks one card from each pile and places them face up.

☐ Player 1 then has one minute to call out as many numbers as he/she can in the sequence.

☐ **Player 2** records how many correct numbers in the sequence are called out.

☐ Play continues either for one minute or until an incorrect number is called out.

☐ Play then moves to Player 2.

☐ Play continues until all the cards are used.

■ The winner is the player who says the most correct numbers.

Dear Helper
This game will help your child practise number sequences, such as 'add 2'. If your child is finding it difficult to call out the numbers in a sequence, allow them to write the sequence on a piece of paper. As an added challenge, choose larger starting numbers – for example, 120, 134, 178 or 199.

Name   Date

Doubling game

■ It is possible to play this game on your own, but it is more fun with someone else!

☐ Cut out the cards below and shuffle them.

☐ Turn them face down, then take a card and double it.

☐ Your helper then doubles your total, then you double theirs, and so on.

☐ The first player to get past 100 wins a point.

☐ Pick another card and start again.

☐ Write down what numbers you make.

■ The winner is the player with the most points when you have used all the cards.

1	2	3	4
5	6	7	8
9	10	11	12
13	14	15	16

Dear Helper
The point of this game is for your child to practise recalling doubles that they already know, and to increase their speed and efficiency with more difficult ones where the number has to be partitioned (split). For example, double 37 = double 30 + double 7 = 60 + 14 = 74. Look for realistic answers. You could also remind your child to check that their answers are realistic by estimating – for example, double 37 will be more than double 35 and less than double 40. If your child can complete this task easily, alter the number cards to make them into two- or three-digit numbers and aim for a total of 500.

Name   Date

BLOCK B

Speed test for 4- and 8-times tables

◾ You will need a stopwatch for this activity.

◾ Time yourself, or ask someone to time you, to complete this 4-times table test.

$4 \times 4 =$ ⬜ $1 \times 4 =$ ⬜

$8 \times 4 =$ ⬜ $3 \times 4 =$ ⬜

$2 \times 4 =$ ⬜ $9 \times 4 =$ ⬜

$5 \times 4 =$ ⬜ $10 \times 4 =$ ⬜

$7 \times 4 =$ ⬜ $6 \times 4 =$ ⬜

◾ What was your time?

◾ Did you get them all correct? If not, do the test again.

◾ The 8-times table is actually double the 4-times table.

◾ Use this knowledge to help you with this 8-times table test.

$3 \times 8 =$ ⬜ $2 \times 8 =$ ⬜

$8 \times 8 =$ ⬜ $10 \times 8 =$ ⬜

$1 \times 8 =$ ⬜ $6 \times 8 =$ ⬜

$5 \times 8 =$ ⬜ $4 \times 8 =$ ⬜

$7 \times 8 =$ ⬜ $9 \times 8 =$ ⬜

◾ What was your time?

◾ Now do both tests again.

◾ Try to beat your record for each one.

◾ Make sure you get all the answers correct!

Dear Helper
This activity helps your child to revise their 4- and 8-times tables. Ideally, you should time your child so that they can concentrate on doing the tests. Encourage them to recall the answers as quickly as possible; hopefully, once remembered they will never be forgotten!

Name	Date

Shape sifting

🔲 Tick the polygons that are irregular.

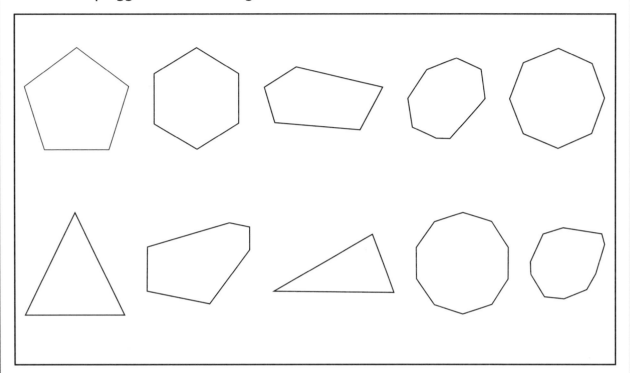

🔲 Tick the shapes that have two lines of symmetry.

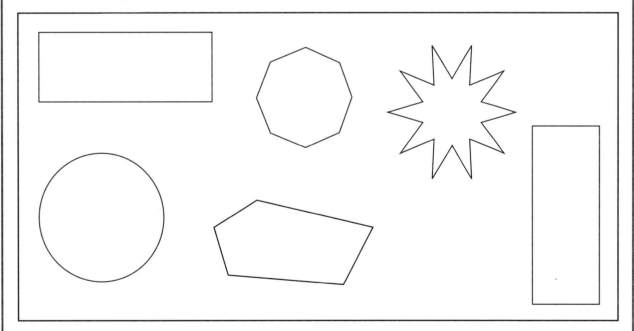

Dear Helper
This activity helps your child to recognise regular and irregular polygons and to find lines of symmetry in 2D shapes. Your child could practise drawing 2D shapes on the back of this sheet. Encourage them to use a ruler and be accurate with their measurements. Squares and rectangles should be quite straightforward but children may need a little help with regular shapes with five or more sides.

BLOCK B

Name	Date

What makes the box?

🔳 Tick the nets that would form a cube.

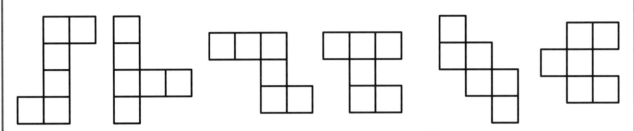

🔳 Draw a possible net of this chocolate box in the space below.

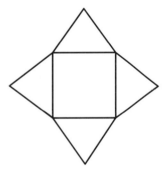

🔳 Which 3D shape would this net form?

Answer _____

Dear Helper
This activity helps your child to visualise 3D objects from 2D drawings (nets). Your child could have some hands-on experience of nets of 3D shapes by exploring un-folded food packaging such as cereal boxes. Take care if using sharp scissors!

Name	Date

Card connect

- Cut out the cards.
- Do this activity with a friend.
  - ☐ Put out the cards (face up) on the table.
  - ☐ One of you chooses a card and reads it out.
  - ☐ The other one finds the card that begins with the answer, then reads out that card.
  - ☐ Repeat this until all the cards have been used.

30 + 40	70 – 20	50 + 160	210 – 120	90 + 80
170 – 20	150 + 80	230 – 50	180 + 10	190 – 60
130 + 90	220 – 80	140 + 110	250 – 170	80 + 190
270 – 30	240 + 60	300 – 180	120 + 80	200 – 40
160 + 130	290 – 30	260 + 20	280 – 180	100 + 10
110 – 90	20 + 20	40 – 30	10 + 50	60 – 30

Dear Helper

This activity helps your child to use known addition and subtraction facts and their understanding of place value to calculate sums and differences of multiples of 10. Please do the activity together, taking turns to find the next card. For example, for 30 + 40 your child could work out 3 + 4 to find out that there are seven tens in total, making the answer 70. If this is too difficult for some of the larger numbers, ask your child to try using a pencil-and-paper method. Challenge them to try the activity again, but time how long it takes to complete. How quickly can you do it together?

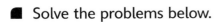
BLOCK B

Name	Date

Sums and products

■ Solve the problems below.

   ☐ Write your answer.

   ☐ Write a sentence to show how you worked it out.

1. What numbers have a sum of 14 and a product of 48? _____

2. What numbers have a sum of 16 and a product of 63? _____

3. What numbers have a sum of 10 and a product of 25? _____

4. What numbers have a sum of 11 and a product of 24? _____

5. What numbers have a sum of 13 and a product of 42? _____

6. What numbers have a sum of 13 and a product of 36? _____

■ Make up your own number problem like the ones above.

   ☐ Write it on the back of this sheet.

   ☐ Now ask your helper or a friend to solve it!

Dear Helper
Children tend to make up very hard problems when challenging adults, so it's OK to ask the child to show you how to solve their number problem. Make sure your child brings their number problem back to school for their friends to try in class.

Name   Date

Times-tables investigation

■ Investigate the following statement by trying out lots of examples to decide if it is true:

If a number is in the 10-times table, it is also in the 2-times and the 5-times tables.

■ Complete this sentence. (Circle true or false.)

☐ I think the statement is true / false because:

_____

_____

_____

_____

Dear Helper
This homework aims to help your child investigate a general statement. They could start by writing out the 10-times table and then write out the 2- and the 5-times tables to compare them. Ask them to take back to school everything they write down while working on this investigation. As a challenge you could ask your child to think up a similar statement about other times tables, such as the 6-, 3- and 4-times tables.

Name	Date

Double dice

■ **A game for two people.** You will need two dice.

Game 1: Start by using only one dice. Throw the dice and take turns to double the number until one of you bridges 100. That person gains a point. Record the results below. Repeat this five more times.

Number thrown	Double	Double	Double	Double	Double	Double	Double	Winner

Game 2: Throw two dice twice. Arrange the digits to make two two-digit numbers that are quite close together. For example: 6, 4, 2 and 5 can be arranged to make 46 and 52.

☐ Use the near double to add the two numbers together, adjusting the answer: 46 + 46 = 92, then 92 + 6 = 98, so 46 + 52 = 98.

☐ Record this addition in the table below.

☐ Play four times and add up your totals. The player with the higher score wins.

Numbers	Double	Adjust

Dear Helper

Your child should use these games to practise a variety of strategies for adding. Doubles and near doubles are useful tools for adding mentally or with some informal jottings. You can help your child by encouraging them to learn all of the doubles of numbers to 50, and the corresponding halves. You could do this by making a list and reciting the doubles, then the halves.

Name	Date

What a thing to say!

◖ This maths teacher has got his notes mixed up. Some of his statements are true and some are nonsense!

◖ Identify the statements that are true by ticking the correct box.

◖ You can test out the statements by making notes on the back of this sheet.

1. The sum of two even numbers is always even.　True ☐　　False ☐

2. The sum of two odd numbers is always odd.　True ☐　　False ☐

3. The sum of an even number and an odd number is sometimes even and sometimes odd.　True ☐　　False ☐

4. Three rights make a wrong.　True ☐　　False ☐

5. The sum of three even numbers is always even.　True ☐　　False ☐

6. Multiples of 10 always end with a zero.　True ☐　　False ☐

7. Multiples of 5 can only end with a 5.　True ☐　　False ☐

8. Multiples of 4 will always be even.　True ☐　　False ☐

9. Pigs have wings and can fly.　True ☐　　False ☐

10. Odd numbers, when doubled, become even.　True ☐　　False ☐

Dear Helper
This activity helps your child to practise reasoning and explaining as they investigate whether mathematical statements are true or false. Ask them to explain to you the thinking behind their answers. Your child could continue this activity on the back of this sheet by writing five statements of their own, one of which is false. They could then challenge you to identify the false one! Ask them to explain to you their thinking about their statements.

BLOCK B

Name	Date

Factors

■ Put an X on the factors of the numbers in the middle of each big X.

Dear Helper
This activity helps your child to revise their times tables. By the end of Year 4, children are expected to know and recall all the multiplication facts, or times tables, up to 10 × 10. If your child is still having difficulty, put aside a few minutes each day to fill in the gaps in their knowledge.

Handling data and measures

Activity name	Learning objectives	Managing the homework
C1		
Converting lengths Practise metric conversions.	Choose and use standard metric units and their abbreviations when estimating, measuring and recording length; know the meaning of kilo, centi and milli, and, where appropriate, use decimal notation to record measurements (for example, 1.3m)	**Before:** Ask the children questions such as: *How many millimetres in a centimetre? How many centimetres in a metre?* **After:** Review the sheet together. Invite some children from each ability group to suggest answers.
What will you use? Suggest what equipment and units to use to measure the given items.	Choose and use standard metric units and their abbreviations when estimating, measuring and recording length; know the meaning of kilo, centi and milli, and, where appropriate, use decimal notation to record measurements (for example, 1.3m)	**Before:** Ask questions such as: *How would you measure the length of the floor? What units would you use?* **After:** Review the sheet together. Discuss suggestions that children make for measuring equipment and units.
The shortest distance Find the shortest distance across a grid.	Choose and use standard metric units and their abbreviations when estimating, measuring and recording length; know the meaning of kilo, centi and milli, and, where appropriate, use decimal notation to record measurements (for example, 1.3m)	**Before:** Review how to change millimetres to centimetres, centimetres to metres. **After:** Invite solutions from children from each ability group. Discuss how the children totalled the measurements.
Reading rulers Measure objects without starting from 0cm on a ruler.	Interpret intervals and divisions on partially numbered scales and record readings accurately, where appropriate to the nearest tenth of a unit	**Before:** Discuss the units we use for measurement. **After:** Compare answers and go through an example with the class.
C2		
Favourite days Answer some questions from a bar chart to show the most popular day of the school week.	Answer a question by identifying what data to collect; organise, present, analyse and interpret the data in tables, diagrams, tally charts, pictograms and bar charts, using ICT where appropriate	**Before:** Discuss how to take readings from a bar chart. **After:** Compare answers. Discuss question 5 on the worksheet: *Why do you think Wednesday could be a popular day of the week?* This cannot be established from the graph, so children should guess - for example, it could be a day the class has PE.
Parts of a litre A matching activity to revise the corresponding parts of a litre.	Choose and use standard metric units and their abbreviations when estimating, measuring and recording weight; know the meaning of kilo, centi and milli, and, where appropriate, use decimal notation to record measurements (for example, 0.6 kg)	**Before:** Recap equivalent measures (for example, 500ml = ½ litre = 0.5 litre). **After:** Compare and discuss the children's answers.
Bar charts Present information in a bar chart and answer questions about it.	● Organise, present, analyse and interpret the data in tables, diagrams, tally charts, pictograms and bar charts, using ICT where appropriate ● Suggest a line of enquiry and the strategy needed to follow it; collect, organise and interpret selected information to find answers	**Before:** Remind the children how to complete a bar chart. **After:** Look at any examples that the children have done at home.
Reading scales Look at scales on measuring jugs with different intervals of step size.	Compare the impact of representations where scales have intervals of differing step size	**Before:** Look at the different scales used on items of measuring equipment. **After:** Ask the class to discuss their experiences of measuring quantities of water at home.

Handling data and measures

Activity name	Learning objectives	Managing the homework
C3		
Carroll families Use a Carroll diagram to investigate the statement 'Most people over the age of 15 own a mobile phone'.	Answer a question by identifying what data to collect; organise, present, analyse and interpret the data in tables, diagrams, tally charts, pictograms and bar charts, using ICT where appropriate	**Before:** Remind the children how to fill in a Carroll diagram. **After:** Discuss the findings and the statement.
Workout pictograms Complete a pictogram, then redraw it to a different scale, using pencil and paper or a computer.	Answer a question by identifying what data to collect; organise, present, analyse and interpret the data in tables, diagrams, tally charts, pictograms and bar charts, using ICT where appropriate	**Before:** Stress to the children that the aim is to present the data as clearly as possible. Discuss the layout of the pictogram and the use of keys and labels. **After:** Compare the children's representations.
Battle of the bands Place information into a Venn diagram.	• Suggest a line of enquiry and the strategy needed to follow it; collect, organise and interpret selected information to find answers • Answer a question by identifying what data to collect; organise, present, analyse and interpret the data in tables, diagrams, tally charts, pictograms and bar charts, using ICT where appropriate	**Before:** Show an example of a Venn diagram and remind the children how to complete one. **After:** Go through the answers with the class.
Music survey Answer questions about data shown in a pictogram.	• Report solutions to puzzles and problems, giving explanations and reasoning orally and in writing, using diagrams and symbols • Organise, present, analyse and interpret the data in tables, diagrams, tally charts, pictograms and bar charts, using ICT where appropriate	**Before:** Remind the children about pictograms, particularly about checking the value of each symbol used. **After:** Go through the questions with the class but give the symbol a higher value.

Name	Date

Converting lengths

◾ Complete this chart.

☐ millimetres = 1 centimetre

☐ centimetres = 1 metre

☐ metres = 1 kilometre

◾ Write the lengths in the new units.

20mm	=	cm	45cm	=	mm
10cm	=	m	6km	=	m
3m	=	cm	8m	=	cm
200m	=	km	400mm	=	cm
70cm	=	mm	350cm	=	m

Dear Helper

This activity gives your child practice in converting length measurements into different units. If your child finds this difficult, talk together about how many of one unit there are in the other. The chart at the top will help with this. Challenge your child to write some conversions for more complicated measures, such as converting 956cm into metres (9.56m), and so on.

Name	Date

What will you use?

- ◣ Look at each picture.

- ◣ Imagine that you have to measure what is in the picture.

- ◣ Write underneath which measuring equipment you would use (ruler, metre stick or measuring tape).

- ◣ Write which units you would use.

I would measure this
with a _____
I would use
_____ units.

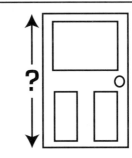

I would measure this
with a _____
I would use
_____ units.

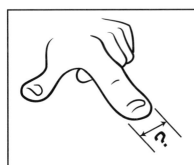

I would measure this
with a _____
I would use
_____ units.

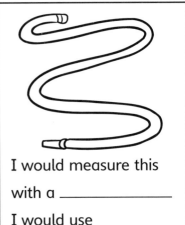

I would measure this
with a _____
I would use
_____ units.

I would measure this
with a _____
I would use
_____ units.

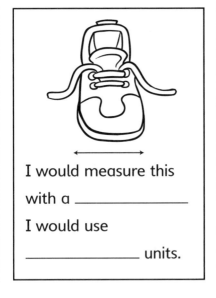

I would measure this
with a _____
I would use
_____ units.

Dear Helper
This activity helps your child to remember that the range of measuring equipment has different uses, and that the appropriate standard units need to be chosen for the size of what is measured. If your child is unsure about which units to use, discuss the size of a unit. Your child can then make a good estimate of which to choose. Challenge your child to think of more things that could be measured for length, what to measure them with, and the units to use. They could write this on the back of this sheet.

BLOCK C

Name   Date

The shortest distance

■ Find the shortest distance across this grid.

■ You may move horizontally or vertically.

Start

120cm	8m	2m	500cm	24m
400cm	1.5m	17m	420cm	345cm
40mm	56cm	184cm	12.5m	320cm

Finish

Dear Helper

This activity helps your child to total measurements. These measurements are in different units, so it would be helpful to change these into the same unit where possible. If your child finds this difficult, do this together, discussing how many millimetres make a centimetre, and so on. Challenge your child to find the longest route. They may use a calculator if they wish.

Name	Date

Reading rulers

■ Read the length of the worms to the nearest millimetre. In each case, the tip of the worm's tail is at the 0cm mark on the ruler.

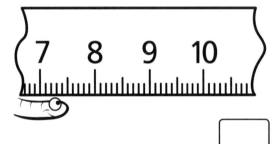

☐ cm

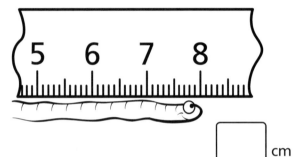

☐ cm

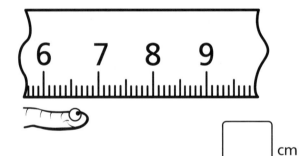

☐ cm

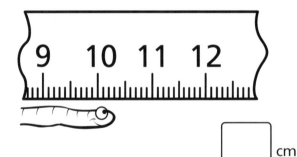

☐ cm

Dear Helper
This activity helps your child to practise measuring lengths. Let your child measure objects around the house with a ruler. Make sure they start the measurement from the zero mark and not the 1cm point. Encourage them to hold the ruler steadily and to double check their measurements.

Name   Date

Favourite days

◀ Look at the bar chart and answer the following questions.

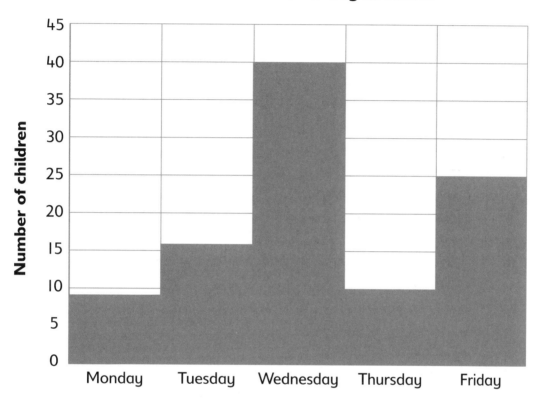

100 children's favourite day at school

Day of the week

1. How many children took part in the survey?

2. What was the favourite day of the week?

3. Which day of the week did ten children vote for?

4. What is the difference between the number of votes for Thursday and the number of votes for Wednesday?

5. Why do you think Wednesday could be a popular day of the week?

6. If 16 children voted Tuesday as their favourite day of the week, how many children voted Monday as their favourite day?

Dear Helper

This graph is called a bar chart, on which the intervals have been labelled in 5s. Your child will find it easy to read off the intervals of 5 and 10 (Wednesday and Friday), but will find it more difficult to read the results for Monday and Tuesday. Encourage your child to make an estimate when only part of the rectangle is shaded (remind them that each rectangle/interval on the bar chart represents five children). As an extra challenge, ask your child to redraw this bar chart using intervals of 2, or to try to draw a bar chart on a computer if one is available.

Name   Date

Parts of a litre

■ You will need some coloured pencils for this activity.

■ Look at the cans and bottles below and see if you can colour those with the same capacities in the same colour.

■ Now look in your store cupboard or fridge at home. Can you find any packaging with the same capacity?

Dear Helper
This activity should help reinforce the equivalent ways of writing capacities, using fractions and decimals. Encourage your child to think of the largest capacities and find the matching pair (or more) and then the smallest. If possible, match up some of the capacities with packaging of cartons or cans from home so that the child starts to visualise the 'size' of each capacity. Making different piles of the equivalent measures as you find them will help with this. As an extra challenge ask: *Which ways can you write 10.5 litres? ...20¼ litres? ...100.75 litres?*

Name	Date

Bar charts

◼ The table below shows how many people came to the Lunch Counter restaurant during one week.

Monday	60
Tuesday	55
Wednesday	15
Thursday	80
Friday	25
Saturday	90
Sunday	45

◼ Draw a bar chart to show this information. Give your bar chart a title.

Title _____

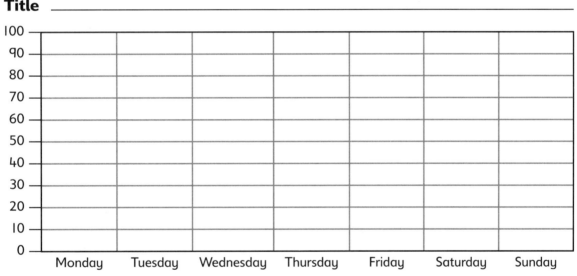

1. On which day did the Lunch Counter have the most customers?

2. Which was the least busy day?

3. Which was the fourth busiest day?

4. Which two days had a total of 145 customers?

5. How many customers were there over the weekend?

6. On the back of this sheet write three sentences about the bar chart, using the words 'most', 'least' and 'difference'.

BLOCK C

Dear Helper

This activity helps your child to organise, display and interpret information to find answers to questions. Encourage your child to label the bar chart and see that it has a title. To extend this activity, look in newspapers, magazines and reference books for information that your child could present in a bar chart. Sports results are a good source of data. Your child could investigate questions such as: 'How many goals did [their favourite team] score each season over the last ten years?'

Name   Date

Reading scales

■ Luke has 650ml of orange juice. He pours it into three different containers.

■ Draw the level of juice in each one.

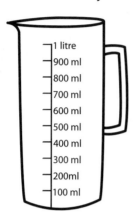
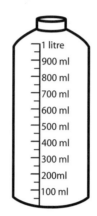
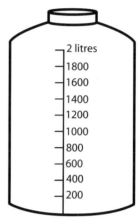

■ Justine has 350ml of apple juice. She poured it into three different containers.

■ Draw the level of juice in each one.

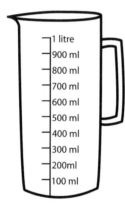
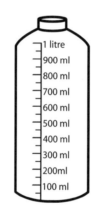
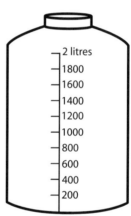

■ Ahmed has a 330ml carton of milk. He poured it into three different containers.

■ Draw the level of milk in each one.

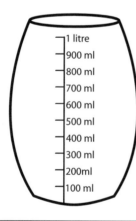
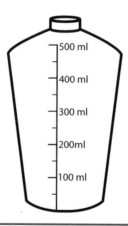
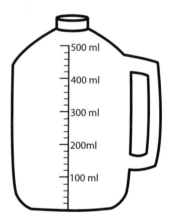

Dear Helper

This activity helps your child to practise reading scales on measuring jugs. Use a measuring jug to measure quantities of water at the kitchen sink. Start with round numbers such as 200ml, 400ml and so on, then try to measure as accurately as possible, to the nearest millilitre, with the scale used on the jug.

Name   Date

Carroll families

◼ Write the names of ten people from your family, friends or neighbours in the correct positions on the Carroll diagram below.

	Owns a mobile phone	**Does not own a mobile phone**
15 years old or younger		
Not 15 years old or younger		

◼ Use this information to help you decide if the following statement is true or false:

Most people in the UK over 15 years of age own a mobile telephone.

True / False

◼ Take your completed sheet into school so that you can discuss your findings with the rest of your class.

Dear Helper
This activity aims to show your child that a Carroll diagram can be used to organise information. If you cannot find ten people locally to survey, perhaps your child could think of friends or members of their family who they know fit into one of the boxes. As an extra challenge ask: *How else could you sort this information?*

BLOCK C

Name	Date

Workout pictograms

■ This pictogram shows the number of hours of exercise 100 children took in one week.

■ Fill in the '4 hours or more' row. Remember that all the rows must add up to 100 in total.

<table>
<tr><td rowspan="5">Hours</td><td></td><td>☺ = 5 children</td></tr>
<tr><td>Less than 1 hour</td><td>☺☺</td></tr>
<tr><td>Less than 2 hours</td><td>☺☺☺☺</td></tr>
<tr><td>Less than 3 hours</td><td>☺☺☺☺☺☺</td></tr>
<tr><td>Less than 4 hours</td><td>☺☺☺</td></tr>
<tr><td></td><td>4 hours or more</td><td></td></tr>
<tr><td></td><td></td><td>Number of children</td></tr>
</table>

■ Now, using the data in the pictogram, complete the blank pictogram below to represent the same data using the scale ☺ = 10 children.

  ☐ Remember that you may have to use half a ☺ to represent 5 children.

  ☐ The main aim is to make your results very clear for the reader. You may use a computer if you like.

■ At school you will be comparing your presentation with the others in your class.

☺ = 10 children

Hours		Number of children
	Less than 1 hour	
	Less than 2 hours	
	Less than 3 hours	
	Less than 4 hours	
	4 hours or more	

Dear Helper

This activity reinforces work that your child has been doing on handling data. Your child has been taught how to draw pictograms and bar charts, and how to use a computer to present data. Encourage them to take plenty of time and use most of the space on the page to make their pictograms as clear as possible for the reader.

Name	Date

Battle of the bands

◀ DJ MC Squared did a survey to find out who preferred either of two groups in his 'Battle of the bands' competition.

◀ Here are his results.

Preferred The Belles	Preferred Spider	Both	Neither
//// //// //	//// ///	////	//// /

◀ Put the information into the Venn diagram shown below.

Battle of the bands

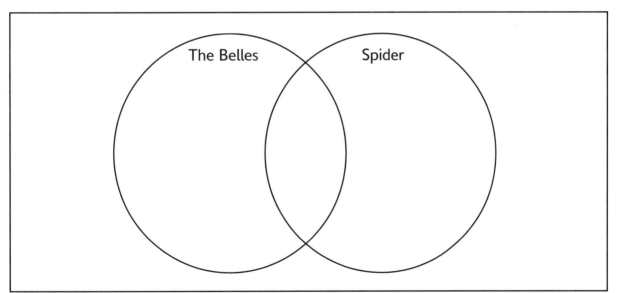

Dear Helper
This activity helps your child to practise organising information in Venn diagrams. If your child is unfamiliar with Venn diagrams, they will need your help with this one. This is a simple introduction and once the information has been studied carefully the process should be straightforward. Ask your child questions about the data when the Venn diagram is completed.

Name	Date

Music survey

■ DJ MC Squared drew a pictogram showing the number of people who liked different types of music.

■ Here are his results. Each CD symbol represents two people.

Type of music	Number of people
Rock	◉ ◉ ◉ ◉ ◉ ◉ ◉ ◉ ◉
Hip hop	◉ ◉ ◉ ◉ ◉ ◉
Country	◉ ◉ ◉
Classic	◉ ◉ ◉ ◉ ◉ ◉ ◉
Jazz	◉ ◉ ◉ ◉

1. Which was the most popular type of music? _____

2. Which was the least popular type of music? _____

3. How many more people liked hip hop than jazz? _____

4. How many people liked classic and jazz in total? _____

5. How many people did MC Squared ask altogether? _____

Dear Helper
This activity helps your child to interpret data presented in a pictogram. Encourage your child to read the information carefully first before answering the questions. Remember that each symbol represents two people. You could extend this activity by changing the value of the symbol.

Calculating, measuring and understanding shape

Activity name	Learning objectives	Managing the homework
D1		
Money, money, money! Solve some short word problems.	Solve one-step and two-step problems involving numbers, money or measures, including time; choose and carry out appropriate calculations	**Before:** Explain that the children are not allowed to use a calculator for these problems and that they should write down how they worked out their answers. **After:** Ask the children what methods they used to solve the problems.
Time snap A 'Snap' game to practise reading times on analogue and digital clocks.	Read time to the nearest minute; use am, pm and 12-hour clock notation	**Before:** Review reading times from analogue and digital clocks to the nearest minute, **After:** Play the 'Snap' game with the class in two teams. It would be helpful to use an enlarged set of cards for this.
Estimating and measuring mass Estimate masses and collect labels from food packets showing mass.	Choose and use standard metric units and their abbreviations when estimating, measuring and recording weight; know the meaning of kilo, centi and milli, and, where appropriate, use decimal notation to record measurements (for example, 0.6kg)	**Before:** Discuss what sorts of packets would be suitable to measure, and how to use scales. Invite the children to bring in some suitable examples of empty packaging if possible. **After:** Discuss what types of scales the children found at home. Look at the different packaging they brought back into the classroom: is the mass clearly displayed?
Shapes and coordinates Draw shapes of squares and rectangles with particular areas and perimeters onto a grid and record their coordinates.	Describe and identify the position of a square [and other shapes] on a grid of squares	**Before:** Try the first question together to ensure that the children realise there are different answers that can all be correct. **After:** Share the children's different answers.
D2		
Talk time Look at a telephone bill at home with an adult and work out an approximate per-minute charge for a call.	Solve one-step and two-step problems involving numbers, money or measures, including time; choose and carry out appropriate calculations, using calculator methods where appropriate	**Before:** Talk about what information to look for on a utility bill. Give an example of how to find the cost of the calls and then divide by the number of minutes. If you have time, prepare a 'pretend' phone bill to send home with the children, so that they all have the same answers to find. **After:** Compare costs and check answers.
Bright white Investigate the costs of different types of toothpaste.	Solve one-step and two-step problems involving numbers, money or measures, including time; choose and carry out appropriate calculations	**Before:** Discuss 'finding the difference' and revise how to multiply by 10. **After:** Compare the children's findings. Ask: *Which toothpaste was the best value for money? How much could the family save over a year?*
Following directions Follow instructions to draw a route on a piece of A4 paper.	Recognise horizontal and vertical lines	**Before:** Recap horizontal, vertical, clockwise, anticlockwise, right, left, 180° and 90° turns. **After:** Share the children's drawings with the class and discuss what was the most difficult part of the task.
Calculating answers Use mental arithmetic skills and the grid method to multiply two-digit numbers by a single-digit number.	• Derive and recall multiplication facts up to 10 × 10, the corresponding division facts and multiples of numbers to 10 up to the tenth multiple • Develop and use written methods to record, support and explain multiplication of two-digit numbers by a one-digit number (for example, 15 × 9)	**Before:** Go through a multiplication question on the board using the grid method. **After:** Go through the answers with the class. Ensure that everyone is comfortable with the grid method of calculation.

BLOCK D

Calculating, measuring and understanding shape

Activity name	Learning objectives	Managing the homework
D3		
Angle grinding Order angles of different sizes and find examples of angles less than 90°.	Know that angles are measured in degrees and that one whole turn is 360°; draw, compare and order angles less than 180°	**Before:** Talk through the numbering of the angles on the sheet. **After:** Go through the answers and share the locations/objects where the children found angles less than 90°.
Estimating and measuring capacity Estimate capacities and collect labels from food packets showing capacity.	Choose and use standard metric units and their abbreviations when estimating, measuring and recording capacity; know the meaning of kilo, centi and milli, and, where appropriate, use decimal notation to record measurements (for example, 0.6kg)	**Before:** Discuss how to use a measuring jug and which sorts of packets would be suitable to measure and bring in to school. **After:** Look at packaging the children have brought in. Ask: *Is the capacity clearly displayed?*
Trans-Air challenge Use an airline timetable to answer questions.	Read time to the nearest minute; use am, pm and 12-hour clock notation; choose units of time to measure time intervals; calculate time intervals from timetables	**Before:** Review and discuss how to work out time durations from the timetable. **After:** Look at the timetable. Ask: *How many hours does the Trans-Air plane spend in the air each week?*
Money columns Practise column addition involving money, using decimal notation.	Refine and use efficient written methods to add two-digit and three-digit whole numbers	**Before:** Recap how to set out addition calculations involving money using squared paper. If appropriate, set a limit on the number of calculations and combinations to be found. **After:** Compare answers and check that the children were able to find an appropriate number of calculations.

SCHOLASTIC

Name   Date

Money, money, money!

■ Use any method you like (but not a calculator) to answer these questions. Show your workings.

1. A CD costs £9.99. Sundeep gets 50p a week for pocket money. How many weeks will it take Sundeep to save enough money to buy a CD?

2. It costs £1.20 for a child to go to the cinema. How much will it cost for six children to go to the cinema?

3. When I went shopping last week I bought three books. Each book cost £5.99. How much change did I get from £20?

4. A large fruit bar costs 65p. How many bars could I buy if I had £3?

BLOCK D

Dear Helper
Solving problems is a very important part of mathematics. Talk to your child about the problems above. Ask whether they need to use +, −, × or ÷ each time. Allow them to solve the problems in any way they see fit. Try to resist the temptation to tell them a 'quicker' way! If your child is really stuck let them use the calculator, but ask them to write down which keys they press.

Name	Date

Time snap

- ◼ Cut up the time pelmanism cards below, to make 20 separate cards.

- ◼ Play this game with a friend.

  - ☐ Shuffle the cards.

  - ☐ Place the cards in a stack, face down.

  - ☐ Take turns to turn over the top card.

  - ☐ Make two piles of turned-over cards.

  - ☐ When the top cards from each pile match, say 'Time snap!'

  - ☐ Whoever says this first, and is correct, takes the cards.

- ◼ The winner is the player with more cards when all the cards have been used.

12:13	7.36	9.08	3.41	11.59

6.27	5.42	4.24	6.23	2.07

Dear Helper

This activity helps your child to read digital and analogue clock faces to the nearest minute. If your child struggles with this, spread out the cards, face up. Ask your child to find two cards that have matching times. Ask them to read the time from the cards. Challenge your child to tell the time at every opportunity, using both analogue and digital clocks around the house and when you are out together.

Name   Date

Estimating and measuring mass

◼ Look at the following questions and circle the amounts that you think are correct.

1. How many letters would weigh approximately 100g?

   1   2   5   10   20

2. How many sheets of A4 paper weigh approximately 100g?

   3   20   50   100   200

3. How many mugs weigh approximately 500g?

   1   2   3   4   5

4. How many tablespoons weigh approximately 500g?

   2   5   10   20   40

◼ Now look in your food cupboard to see if there are any packets with the mass marked on them. Look for a packet that weighs between 100 grams and 500 grams.

◼ Make a note of any you find, or take an empty packet to school to show your teacher.

BLOCK D

Dear Helper

This activity will help your child to understand the relationship between different weights. They have been learning about grams and kilograms at school this week. To support your child, it may help to weigh one object using scales and then use that as a guide for other objects. If this is not possible, find an object that weighs 100g or 500g (a packet or tin that has the weight marked on it) and encourage your child to hold an object in one hand and try to compare it with the 100g or 500g weight in the other hand. As an extra challenge, ask: *How many would I need to make 1kg? ...2kg? ...5kg?*

Name   Date

Shapes and coordinates

◼ Read carefully the three clues provided below.

◼ Draw the shapes onto the grid and then write down the coordinates under the clue. (Remember to use brackets.)

1. I am a square with sides of length 4cm.

_____

2. I am a rectangle with a perimeter of 20cm.

_____

3. I am a rectangle with an area of 15cm².

_____

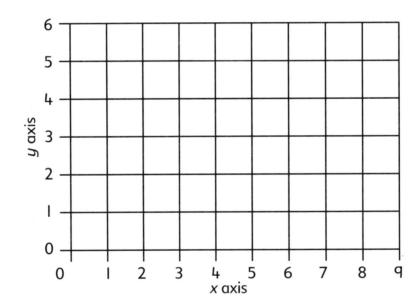

◼ Now make up a clue to another shape that would fit onto the grid.

◼ Write the coordinates of the shape below, and remember what shape it is.

_____

Dear Helper
Your child has been learning how each point on a grid of lines (a point is where the lines cross) can be referred to using numbers such as (2, 3). This is called a 'coordinate pair'. The first number means the number of lines along the grid, and the second number means the number of lines up the grid, so (1, 2) means '1 along and 2 up'. Remind your child that the perimeter is the distance all the way around a shape, and the area is the space inside a shape.

BLOCK D

Name   Date

Talk time

■ Ask an adult to show you a recent telephone bill.

■ Work out the answers to the following questions.

1. What are the dates covered by the phone bill?
   (Hint: it is usually for one or three months) _____

                                                    to _____

2. What is the total cost of the telephone bill?
   Round this amount to the nearest £1.00. _____

3. How many minutes did your household
   spend on the phone during this time? _____
   Round this amount to the nearest ten minutes. _____

4. Now work out an approximation of the cost of a call per minute.
   Divide the total cost by the number of minutes.

   Show how you worked this out here. Ignore any remainders.

Dear Helper
This activity should help your child to see that the skills they are learning at school about problem solving will be useful in life. At school they will be looking at the calculations involved and will be comparing the cost of calls per minute. If you feel uncomfortable about your bill being used in this way, please 'doctor' the bill or prepare a 'pretend' bill. It would be helpful for you to talk through the bill with your child so that they understand that bills come every quarter and that there are charges such as line rental as well as the cost of calls. For extra support, highlight or underline information as you talk it through. As an extra challenge, ask: *If this is a typical phone bill, how much would I pay in a whole year?*

BLOCK D

Name   Date

Bright white

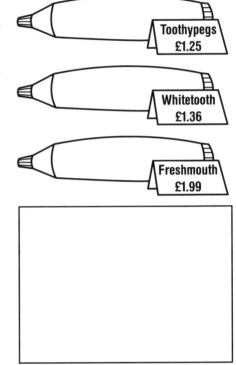

Toothypegs
£1.25

Whitetooth
£1.36

Freshmouth
£1.99

- Look in your local supermarket or shop to find out the price of another tube of toothpaste.

- Draw a picture of the toothpaste tube in the box provided and add the price to the tag.

- Investigate the differences in the prices of the different tubes of toothpaste. Write your results below.

_____.

_____

_____

- Imagine that a family of four uses ten tubes of toothpaste in a year.

- How much could they save in a year by using the cheapest toothpaste rather than the most expensive?

- Write your results and workings below.

Dear Helper
This activity covers word problems involving numbers and money in real-life situations. Encourage your child to record their results logically, comparing two toothpastes before looking at another pair, and to write down everything that they observe or find out. If visiting the shop or supermarket, observe the differences in price of 'branded' toothpastes and the shop's own brand. A more complex challenge would involve comparing different sizes of tubes or packaging, the quantity of toothpaste and prices. For example: *Is toothpaste cheaper in tubes or in pump dispensers?*

Name	Date

Following directions

■ To do this activity you must be sitting down with a pencil and a blank piece of A4 paper in front of you.

■ Ask an adult to make sure that your piece of paper is portrait way up in front of you.

■ Then ask them to read out the following instructions, ONCE ONLY.

   ☐ Turn your paper around 90 degrees.

   ☐ Draw a horizontal line across the middle of the page, so that your page is divided in half.

   ☐ In the top right-hand corner of the page draw a circle.

   ☐ Draw a vertical line from the circle to the middle of the page.

   ☐ Write your name in the bottom right-hand corner of the page.

   ☐ Turn your page around 90 degrees so that the circle is at the bottom of the page.

   ☐ Draw a square on the right-hand side of the page.

   ☐ Turn the page 180 degrees.

   ☐ Draw a horizontal line from one corner of the square to the line in the middle of the page.

   ☐ Now turn your sheet 90 degrees clockwise.

   ☐ Now put your pencil down.

■ Ask the adult to re-read the instructions, going through each step carefully.

■ How good were you at following instructions?

■ Take your picture to school and compare it with your friends' pictures.

Dear Helper

This activity encourages your child to listen to and follow instructions. Make sure that you do not repeat any of the instructions until your child has put their pen down. Before your child starts, it may help to revise the words horizontal (across the page), vertical (up/down the page), 90° (a ¼ turn), 180° (a ½ turn), clockwise/anticlockwise, left and right. As an extra challenge you could include some extra instructions such as: *Draw a triangle in the bottom left-hand corner* or *Draw a star in the square*. For checking purposes, note down any extra instructions that you give.

Name	Date

Calculating answers

◾ Use your mental arithmetic skills to answer these questions.

3 × 8 = ☐   30 ÷ 6 = ☐

4 × 7 = ☐   64 ÷ 8 = ☐

6 × 5 = ☐   24 ÷ 3 = ☐

5 × 9 = ☐   45 ÷ 9 = ☐

7 × 9 = ☐   12 ÷ 2 = ☐

8 × 7 = ☐   50 ÷ 10 = ☐

◾ Now use the grid method to answer these multiplication questions.

◾ The first one has been done for you.

16 × 4 = ☐

×	10	6	
4	40	24	= 64

26 × 3 = ☐

×			
			=

69 × 2 = ☐

×			
			=

35 × 6 = ☐

×			
			=

73 × 7 = ☐

×			
			=

47 × 4 = ☐

×			
			=

84 × 8 = ☐

×			
			=

58 × 5 = ☐

×			
			=

91 × 9 = ☐

×			
			=

Dear Helper

This activity helps your child to practise the grid method of multiplication they have been taught in school. It is probably a different way to which you were taught! The children are taught formal column-style calculations by the end of Year 6. Encourage your child to use mental strategies in order to make estimates of answers before they use the grid method.

Name	Date

Angle grinding

◼ Number the boxes 1 to 8 in order, starting with the smallest angle.

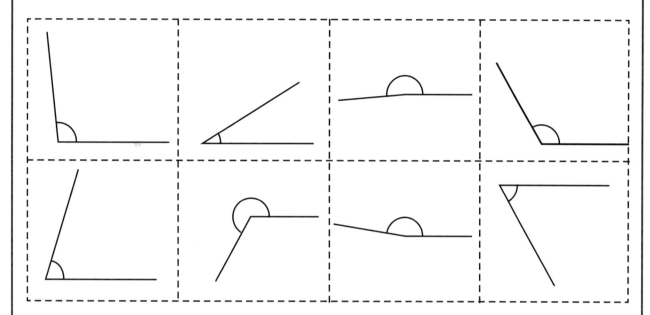

◼ Draw an angle matching the descriptions in the boxes below.

A right angle	Half a right angle	Half of 360 degrees

◼ How would these fit into your ordered angles above?

_____

◼ Challenge: How many angles can you find in your house that are less than
90 degrees? Write on the back of the sheet where you have spotted these.

BLOCK D

Dear Helper
This activity revises what your child has learned about angles: that they are measured in degrees,
that there are 360 degrees in a full turn and 90 degrees in a quarter turn or right angle. Ask: _Is this
angle greater than or less than 90 degrees?_ When your child is looking for angles less than 90 degrees,
suggest that they use the corner of a piece of paper to compare the size of the angles. Angles less than
90 degrees can be found on graters, knives, electrical plugs or on clocks. As an extra challenge, look at a
clock together and ask: _At what times would there be an angle less than 90 degrees between the hands?_

Name   Date

Estimating and measuring capacity

◀ Ask an adult for some help and permission to find the capacity of some household items.

◀ Estimate and measure, in millilitres, the capacity of the following items using water and a measuring jug.

◀ If you do not have an item on the list, cross it out and write in another similar item.

Item	Estimate in millilitres	Capacity in millilitres
A cup		
A mug		
A small bowl		
A small saucepan		
An empty carton or can		

◀ Now look in your food cupboard or fridge to see if there are any packets or bottles with the capacity written on them.

◀ Look for a bottle or can that holds between 100 millilitres and 500 millilitres.

◀ Write the details below or take an empty packet/bottle/can to school to show your teacher.

_____

_____

Dear Helper

This activity will help your child to understand the relationship between different capacities. They have been learning about millilitres and litres at school this week. Estimating is a difficult but important life skill. It may help your child if they find the capacity of one object and then use that as a guide for other objects. Ask: *Will this hold more or less?* As an extra challenge you could estimate, with your child, the capacity of larger items such as a kitchen sink.

BLOCK D

Name	Date

Trans-Air challenge

🔲 Look at the Trans-Air schedule below.

- ☐ It shows the airline's winter flights from London Gatwick to Nice.
- ☐ The planes fly from London Gatwick to Nice, and then turn around and come back again.

Day	Monday	Wednesday	Thursday	Friday	Sunday
Flight No.	PJ203	PJ204	PJ205	PJ206	PJ207
Depart Gatwick	10.05	10.15	10.05	10.00	9.55
Arrive Nice	11.40	11.50	11.40	11.35	11.30
Depart Nice	12.15	12.25	12.10	12.10	12.05
Arrive Gatwick	13.55	14.05	13.55	13.50	13.45

1. How long is the flight from Gatwick to Nice? _____

2. Does it take the same amount of time each day? _____

3. Does it take the same amount of time to fly back to London each day?

_____

4. On which day of the week does it take longer? _____

5. How much longer? _____

6. If I was planning to travel to Nice for the weekend, leaving London on Friday and returning on Sunday, how much time would I spend in the air?

_____

7. If my plane on Sunday was delayed leaving Nice by 25 minutes, at what time would I land at Gatwick?

_____

Dear Helper
This activity will help your child learn how to plan journeys and use timetables in real-life situations. It may be useful to use a ruler or a piece of paper to help your child to read each line of a timetable. As an extra challenge, ask your child to work out how long the Trans-Air plane is in the air each week.

Name   Date

Money columns

- Find the sums of all of the pairs of the following numbers (for example, £13.56 + £8.76, £13.56 + £6.78 and so on – there will be 15 sums in total): £13.56 £8.76 £6.78 £3.14 £2.99 £8.12

- Set out your work using the squared paper below and be sure to keep your decimal points underneath each other, for example:

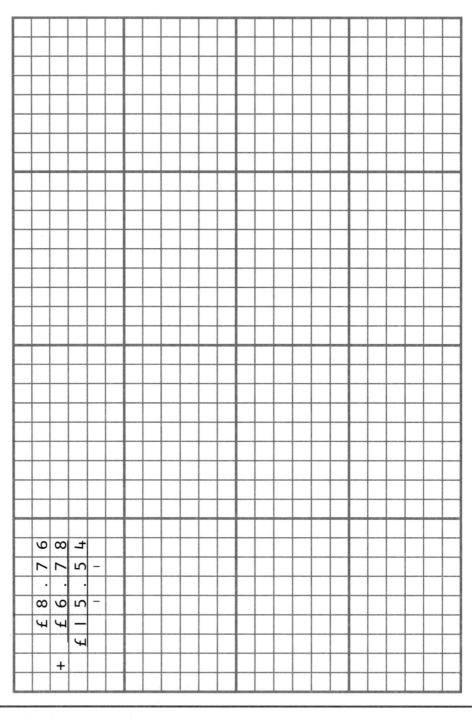

```
   £ 8 . 7 6
 + £ 6 . 7 8
   £15 . 5 4
       1 1
```

Dear Helper

This activity aims to reinforce the work that your child has been doing in class about adding amounts of money in columns. The most important aspect of this is to set out the sum carefully so that the pounds are written beneath the pounds, the pence beneath the pence and the decimal points are directly below each other. Encourage your child to check their calculation with a mental strategy to see if their answer is appropriate, before going on to the next pair. If time allows, challenge your child to find the difference between pairs of numbers. Stress that again the decimal points must line up beneath each other and that the largest amount of money must go on the top (take away the smaller amount from the larger amount).

BLOCK D

Securing number facts, relationships and calculating

Activity name	Learning objectives	Managing the homework
E1		
Times-tables challenge Complete a grid to practise tables facts.	Derive and recall multiplication facts up to 10 × 10, the corresponding division facts and multiples of numbers to 10 up to the tenth multiple	**Before:** Practise reciting the table facts. Ask questions such as: *What is 6 times 5? What is 24 divided by 3?* **After:** Use the grid during a Starter session. Challenge the children to write a fact for each number as you call it out. Keep the pace sharp.
Fraction shapes Describe a smaller shape as a fraction of a larger one.	Find fractions of numbers, quantities or shapes (for example, $^1/_5$ of 30 plums, $^3/_8$ of a 6 × 4 rectangle)	**Before:** On the board, draw a row of two squares, then another row of eight squares, and ask the children to describe the relationship of the smaller row to the larger. **After:** Invite children who have made some more puzzles to draw these on the board for the class to try.
Range of numbers Think of ten different number sentences, using a range of numbers and all four operations.	Represent a puzzle or problem using number sentences, statements or diagrams; use these to solve the problem	**Before:** Talk through the examples given on the worksheet. **After:** Share the number sentences as a class. Ask: *What did you notice about the range of numbers given?* (They are all prime.)
Focus on fractions Look at packets, newspapers and magazines to find examples of fractions.	Find fractions of numbers, quantities or shapes (for example, $^1/_5$ of 30 plums, $^3/_8$ of a 6 × 4 rectangle)	**Before:** Talk about where at home the children might look for examples of fractions. **After:** Discuss the various examples that the children found.
Multiple magic Identify numbers from clues given about their multiples.	Derive and recall multiplication facts up to 10 × 10, the corresponding division facts and multiples of numbers to 10 up to the tenth multiple	**Before:** Remind the children to be logical with their working, and show how writing a list of numbers, then eliminating some, may also help. **After:** Ask: *Which were the numbers? Can you explain why?*
Higher or lower? Colour-code a set of fractions to indicate whether they are greater or less than ½.	Identify equivalent fractions (for example, $^6/_8$ and ¾, $^{70}/_{100}$ and $^7/_{10}$)	**Before:** Order some fractions on a number line marked with 0, ½ and 1. **After:** Review the activity. Ask for other examples of fractions that are greater or less than ½.
E2		
Fraction pelmanism Play an equivalence game with fractions.	Identify equivalent fractions (for example, $^6/_8$ and ¾, $^{70}/_{100}$ and $^7/_{10}$)	**Before:** Review equivalence of the fractions on the worksheet. **After:** Play this as a class game of 'Snap'.
Equivalence snap A game of 'Snap' to practise equivalent fractions.	Identify equivalent fractions (for example, $^6/_8$ and ¾, $^{70}/_{100}$ and $^7/_{10}$)	**Before:** Demonstrate the game to the children. **After:** Go through the answers and check the children's understanding of equivalent fractions.
Dividing codes Colour-code numbers as being divisible by 2, 3, 4, 5 and 10.	Derive and recall multiplication facts up to 10 × 10, the corresponding division facts and multiples of numbers to 10 up to the tenth multiple	**Before:** Recap the various methods of checking that numbers are in the 2-, 3-, 4-, 5- and 10-times tables. Remind the children that if a number is divisible by, for example, 2 and 3 it is also divisible by 6. **After:** Talk through the answers and the methods the children used.
Fractions and decimals Practise matching fractions with equivalent decimals.	Recognise the equivalence between decimal and fraction forms of one half, quarters, tenths and hundredths	**Before:** Remind the class of the meaning of the word 'equivalence' and that a fraction can be expressed as a decimal. **After:** Go through the common fraction/decimal equivalents as stated on the worksheet.

BLOCK E

Securing number facts, relationships and calculating

Activity name	Learning objectives	Managing the homework
Making one Identify fractions that total one whole.	Identify pairs of fractions that total 1	**Before:** Ask the class what you would need to add to one quarter to make one whole. **After:** Go through the answers with the class.
Fractions of shapes Draw shapes and find fractions of them.	Find fractions of numbers, quantities or shapes (for example, $^1/_5$ of 30 plums, $^3/_8$ of a 6 × 4 rectangle)	**Before:** Go through an example on the board. **After:** Look at the drawings the children did and discuss the methods they used in order to be accurate.

E3

Activity name	Learning objectives	Managing the homework
Remaining remainders Answer word problems involving dividing and finding remainders in the context of money and real-life situations.	Develop and use written methods to record, support and explain multiplication and division of two-digit numbers by a one-digit number, including division with remainders (for example, 15 × 9, 98 ÷ 6)	**Before:** Ask the children to think about the number sentence related to the question. **After:** Talk through the answers and methods used to solve each problem.
Are you certain? Investigate remainders that can be made when you divide by 3, 4, 5 and 10.	Develop and use written methods to record, support and explain division of two-digit numbers by a one-digit number, including division with remainders (for example 98 ÷ 6)	**Before:** Remind the children that they need to work logically, and that if a remainder is greater than or equal to the divisor then it can be divided again. **After:** Ask: *Were the statements true? Why?*
Number products Find products using a written method, then find the largest and smallest products.	Develop and use written methods to record, support and explain multiplication of two-digit numbers by a one-digit number (for example, 15 × 9)	**Before:** Recap the various written methods of finding products. **After:** Talk through the answers and the methods the children used.
Decimals equal fractions Colour in sets of equivalent fractions and decimals.	Recognise the equivalence between decimal and fraction forms of one half, quarters, tenths and hundredths	**Before:** Talk through the colour-coding and revise equivalence. **After:** Check equivalent fraction groups.
Finding equivalent fractions Use a fraction grid to find equivalent fractions.	Use diagrams to identify equivalent fractions (for example, $^6/_8$ and ¾, $^{70}/_{100}$ and $^7/_{10}$)	**Before:** Demonstrate how the fraction grid can be used to identify equivalent fractions. **After:** Make a copy of the fraction grid for display in the classroom.
Ratio and proportion Complete statements about ratio and proportion.	Use the vocabulary of ratio and proportion to describe the relationship between two quantities (for example, 'There are 2 red beads to every 3 blue beads, or 2 beads in every 5 beads are red'); estimate a proportion (for example, 'About one quarter of the apples in the box are green')	**Before:** Discuss the meaning of ratio and proportion. **After:** Go through the statements with the class and discuss any issues raised.

BLOCK E

Name	Date

Times-tables challenge

- Ask your helper to time you and check your multiplication or division as you play this game.

  - Choose a square along the start row and say a multiplication or division fact for the number on that square. For example: 5 × 4 = 20.

  - Now move to a square in the next row that touches your previous square (for example: 8 or 45).

  - Say a multiplication or division fact for the number on that square.

  - Repeat this, moving from one square to a touching square in the next row until you reach the finish row.

- How long did this take you?

- Repeat the game, this time trying a different route across the grid.

Start	20	35	16	15	12	50
	8	45	21	70	6	25
	55	30	70	32	45	36
	28	80	16	48	2	90
	35	4	3	27	40	9
Finish	24	14	60	8	100	18

BLOCK E

Dear Helper
Your child is expected to remember multiplication facts for the 2-, 3-, 4-, 5- and 10-times tables. This activity encourages them to practise recall of those facts. For example, if your child begins on 15, they might say 3 × 5 = 15, 5 × 3 = 15, 15 ÷ 3 = 5 or 15 ÷ 5 = 3. Timing your child will help them to realise how well they know these facts. If your child does not know one of the facts, talk about which multiplication table it is likely to come in, and why. Then ask them to say that table until they come to the fact. Challenge your child to see how quickly they can work through all the squares in the grid, and say a fact.

Name   Date

Fraction shapes

◼ Write what fraction the smaller shape is of the larger shape.

Dear Helper
This activity helps your child to recognise fractions of shapes (how much part of a shape is of the whole shape). If your child is uncertain about the fractions, suggest that they cut out the smaller part and place it over the whole so that they can make a direct comparison. Challenge your child to draw some more of these fraction shapes to try out on a friend.

BLOCK E

Name	Date

Range of numbers

■ Use all four operations and the numbers below to make ten different calculations.

☐ The rule is that all answers must be between 50 and 100.

2   3   5   7   11   13   17   19   23   29

☐ Examples: 2 × 29 = 58 or 17 + 19 + 23 = 59.

1. _____

2. _____

3. _____

4. _____

5. _____

6. _____

7. _____

8. _____

9. _____

10. _____

BLOCK E

Dear Helper

This activity encourages your child to look at a range of numbers and make decisions about calculations. To support less confident children, decide on a starting number together and then use add (+) or multiply (×) in order to make a number larger. As an extra challenge, encourage your child to include five calculations using divide (÷) or multiply (×) as part of the sentence.

Name   Date

Focus on fractions

■ Look at home to see how many examples of fractions you can find.

■ Look in the food cupboard or in the newspaper and ask an adult for some ideas.

■ Write, draw or cut out and stick your examples here.

  ☐ Remember to ASK PERMISSION before cutting up any newspaper or magazine!

BLOCK E

Dear Helper
This week your child is looking at fractions. The aim of this activity is to recognise simple fractions that are several parts of a whole so, while your child is looking for examples, it would be useful if you could emphasise the fact that the fractions are not whole things but parts of a whole object or thing. For example, you might cut a pizza into six pieces (sixths) to share. As a challenge, you could ask your child to sort the fractions into those bigger than a half and those smaller than a half.

Name   Date

Multiple magic

■ Find the numbers from the clues below about their multiples.

I am an even number and a multiple of 3. I am less than 10. Who am I? _____	I am an odd multiple of 5. I am less than 20 but greater than 10. Who am I? _____
I am less than 100 but greater than 80. I am a multiple of 10. Who am I? _____	I am a multiple of 4 and 5. I am greater than 40 but less than 80. Who am I? _____
I am an even number. I am a multiple of 3 and 4. I am less than 50. Which numbers could I be? _____	I am an even number. I am greater than 50 but less than 80. I am a multiple of 4. Which numbers could I be? _____
I am a multiple of 2, 3, 4 and 5. What is the smallest number that I could be? _____	I am a multiple of 3 and 5. What is the smallest number that I could be? _____
I am a multiple of 2 and 5. What is the largest two-digit number that I could be? _____	

BLOCK E

Dear Helper

This activity aims to reinforce the work that your child has been doing in school about multiples. A multiple is a number larger than the original number in its times table. So, for example, multiples of 5 are 10, 15, 20, 25, 30 and so on; multiples of 3 are 6, 9, 12, 15, 18 and so on. Encourage your child to write down a list of numbers and then to eliminate them slowly as they work through the clue. For example, for the clue 'I am an even number and a multiple of 3. I am less than 10. Who am I?', encourage your child to write down a list of even numbers that are less than 10 (2, 4, 6, 8) and then to think about which number is in the 3-times table. (Answer: 6.)

Name	Date

Higher or lower?

- ▪ You will need some coloured pencils or pens.
- ▪ Colour these fractions according to the instructions below:
  - ☐ Less than $\frac{1}{2}$ colour in red.
  - ☐ More than $\frac{1}{2}$ colour in yellow.

0.1

0.25

$\frac{7}{10}$

$\frac{3}{8}$

$\frac{1}{5}$

2.5

10.1

$\frac{7}{8}$

$\frac{1}{4}$

$\frac{1}{3}$

$\frac{9}{10}$

0.01

1.25

$\frac{2}{3}$

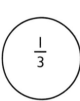
$\frac{3}{4}$

$\frac{1}{10}$

$\frac{4}{5}$

0.6

Dear Helper
This activity will help your child to order fractions and decimals. Encourage them to think about equivalent fractions if they are unsure. Equivalent fractions (such as $^1/_2$ and $^4/_8$) are fractions where the top number and the bottom number of the first fraction have both been multiplied by the same number to make the second fraction. For example: $^1/_4 = {}^2/_8$ where $^1/_4$ multiplied by 2 top and bottom is $^2/_8$. As an extra challenge, ask your child to add other fractions or decimals to the list and colour-code them as greater than or less than $^1/_2$.

BLOCK E

Name   Date

Fraction pelmanism

■ Play this game with a friend.

- ☐ Cut out the cards.
- ☐ Shuffle them.
- ☐ Turn the cards face down on the table.
- ☐ Take turns to pick up two cards.
- ☐ If the two cards are equivalent you keep them.
- ☐ The player to collect the most cards wins.

$\frac{1}{2}$	$\frac{2}{4}$	$\frac{3}{6}$	$\frac{5}{10}$	$\frac{4}{8}$	$\frac{10}{30}$
$\frac{1}{4}$	$\frac{2}{8}$	$\frac{4}{16}$	$\frac{6}{24}$	$\frac{20}{40}$	$\frac{4}{12}$
$\frac{1}{3}$	$\frac{3}{9}$	$\frac{1}{10}$	$\frac{2}{20}$	$\frac{4}{40}$	$\frac{3}{30}$
$\frac{3}{4}$	$\frac{6}{8}$	$\frac{9}{12}$	$\frac{50}{100}$	$\frac{6}{12}$	$\frac{75}{100}$

Dear Helper
This activity helps your child to recognise equivalent fractions, such as $^1/_2$, $^2/_4$, $^4/_8$. Play this game together. If your child does not recognise what the simplest form of the fraction is (for example, that $^{50}/_{100}$ is also $^1/_2$), discuss what the fraction says. For example, $^8/_{12}$ can be said as '8 pieces out of 12'. Talk about how this is the same as 4 out of 6 or 2 out of 3. Challenge your child to say the simplest equivalent form for all the cards.

BLOCK E

Name	Date

Equivalence snap

■ Cut out and play Snap with a helper, using these equivalent fraction cards.

Rules

▢ Cut out the cards, shuffle them and deal them equally between the two players.

▢ **Player 1** starts by laying one of their cards on the table.

▢ **Player 2** then lays one of their cards next to the first card.

▢ Players continue to lay cards on their own piles until two of the cards are equivalent fractions.

▢ If a player spots an equivalent fraction they must shout 'Snap!' The other player then picks up all the cards that are on the table.

▢ The winner is the first player to get rid of all of their cards.

■ Repeat the game, this time a little faster.

$$\frac{1}{2} \quad \frac{2}{4} \quad \frac{8}{16}$$

$$\frac{4}{8} \quad \frac{1}{4} \quad \frac{2}{8}$$

$$\frac{1}{5} \quad \frac{2}{10} \quad \frac{1}{8}$$

$$\frac{2}{16} \quad \frac{1}{10} \quad \frac{2}{20}$$

Dear Helper

Equivalent fractions are fractions such as $^1/_4$ and $^2/_8$ and, where the top and bottom numbers of the smaller fraction have both been multiplied by the same number to make the larger fraction (for example, $^1/_4 \times 2 = ^2/_8$). If your child fails to spot an equivalent fraction, ask them, for example: *What is double 1? What is double 4?* It would also help to move your finger between the two top numbers (numerators) and then between the two bottom numbers (denominators), so that they can spot the connection.

Name	Date

Dividing codes

■ You will need some coloured pens or pencils for this activity.

■ Follow the instructions below.

   ☐ Circle in yellow the numbers that are divisible by 2 and 3.

   ☐ Put a blue box around the numbers that are divisible by 2 and 5.

   ☐ Put a green triangle around the numbers that are divisible 3 and 4.

   ☐ Put a red rectangle around the numbers that are divisible by 4 and 5.

   ☐ Some numbers may have more than one code.

6	12	18	20	36
72	40	45	70	78
60	80	160	30	100
34	56	24	88	90

■ Challenge: Can you think of a number that would be coloured yellow, blue, green and red? Write it below, showing any workings.

BLOCK E

Dear Helper
This activity challenges your child to follow instructions and to think about numbers that are in the 2-, 3-, 4-, 5- and 10-times tables. If your child is finding it difficult to work out, for example, the numbers that are in the 2-times table and then 3-times table, remind them that if a number is in the 2- and 3-times table it will also be in the 6-times table.

Name	Date

Fractions and decimals

■ Draw a line between each fraction in box A and its equivalent decimal in box B.

☐ Be careful, some fractions will link to the same decimal!

Box A	Box B
$\dfrac{1}{100}$	0.3
$\dfrac{2}{8}$	0.01
$\dfrac{4}{16}$	
$\dfrac{27}{100}$	0.5
$\dfrac{1}{2}$	
$\dfrac{7}{14}$	0.9
$\dfrac{1}{10}$	0.25
$\dfrac{1}{4}$	
$\dfrac{3}{10}$	0.63
$\dfrac{6}{12}$	0.27
$\dfrac{9}{10}$	
$\dfrac{63}{100}$	0.1

Dear Helper

This activity helps your child to recognise equivalent fractions and decimals. It will really help your child if they learn these equivalent fractions and decimals off by heart: $\frac{1}{2}$ = 0.5, $\frac{1}{4}$ = 0.25, $\frac{3}{4}$ = 0.75, $\frac{1}{10}$ = 0.1, $\frac{1}{100}$ = 0.01. As a general rule, to write fractions as decimals you change them into tenths and hundredths (for example, $\frac{1}{2}$ = $\frac{5}{10}$ = 0.5; $\frac{1}{4}$ = $\frac{25}{100}$ = 0.25).

Name	Date

Making one

◖ Each of these fractions has a pair which totals 1.

◖ Link them together by drawing a line.

☐ The first one has been done for you.

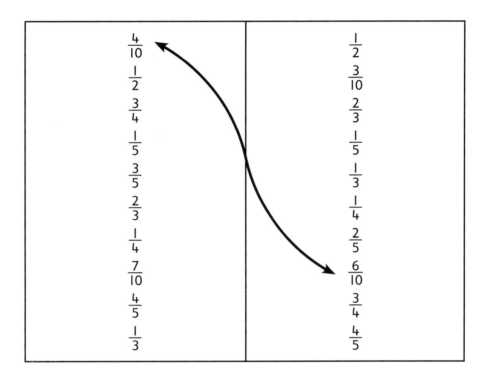

◖ Which fraction would you need to add to each of these to make 1?

1. $\frac{5}{6}$ ☐

2. $\frac{3}{7}$ ☐

3. $\frac{5}{8}$ ☐

4. $\frac{1}{9}$ ☐

Dear Helper

This activity helps your child to identify pairs of fractions that total one whole. Fractions can often prove tricky for children to grasp. You can use everyday objects like dried pasta or buttons to practise finding halves, quarters and other fractions of totals. Ask your child to give you, for example, a quarter of 16 buttons or two fifths of ten pasta shapes.

| Name | Date |

Fractions of shapes

◼ For this activity you will need a ruler and some coloured pencils.

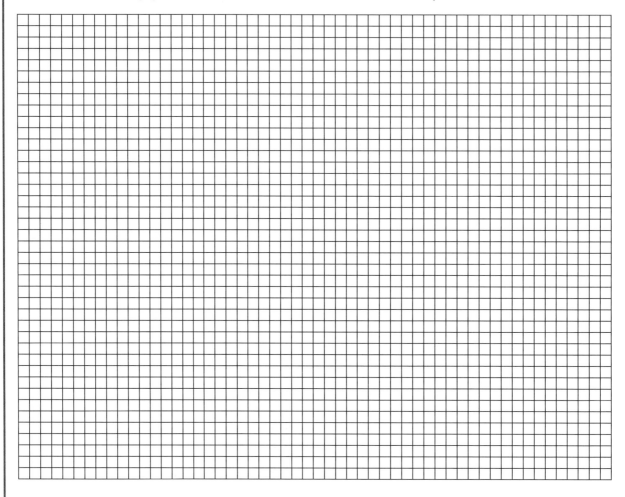

◼ Use a ruler and the grid to draw these shapes, then colour the fractions.

1. A rectangle with $\frac{1}{4}$ blue and $\frac{1}{4}$ red.

2. A square with $\frac{1}{4}$ green and $\frac{1}{8}$ yellow.

3. A hexagon with $\frac{1}{6}$ brown.

4. A rectangle with $\frac{1}{10}$ purple and $\frac{1}{3}$ brown.

5. A rectangle with $\frac{2}{3}$ red.

6. A triangle with $\frac{2}{3}$ blue.

7. A rectangle with $\frac{3}{8}$ green.

Dear Helper
This activity helps your child to practise accurate drawing and finding fractions of shapes. Encourage them to be accurate with their drawings and use the squares on the grid to help them work out the fractions of the shapes.

BLOCK E

Name	Date

Remaining remainders

📖 Work out the following problems, showing all of your working out.

1. I saved some money for a computer game, which cost £45. I saved £4 a month. How long did it take me to save? How much did I have left over?

_____

2. Books cost £5 in a sale. How many books can I buy with £24? How much will I have left?

_____

3. Glue is packed in packs of two tubes. How many packs would I need for 35 tubes of glue?

_____

4. Chairs are stacked in piles of ten. How many piles will 54 chairs give me? How many extra chairs will I need for each pile to equal 10?

_____

5. Tins are sold in packs of four. If I want 23 tins, how many packs of four must I buy and how many will I have left over?

_____

6. I would like to share £26 between ten people. How much will each person receive and how much will be left?

_____

Dear Helper
This activity will help your child to understand that in real life division questions will often involve remainders. Encourage your child to think of a division sentence that will help them and then to try to work out the answers mentally or using jottings. For example, in question 1 your child needs to work out the division sentence 45 ÷ 4. Ask: *What in the 4-times table is near to 45? 44 is 4 x 11 and so 45 ÷ 4 = 11 r1. This is not enough money, so we need another month's money. Then we would have £48. The game cost £45, so it would take 12 months to save and we would have £3 left over.* Challenge your child to think of a question with the answer '4 remainder 4'.

BLOCK E

Name   Date

Are you certain?

1. Paul said, 'When I divide by 3, the only remainders I can get are 1 and 2.'

◧ Investigate this to see if it is true.

☐ Complete this sentence. Circle true or false.

☐ I think the statement is true/false because _____

_____

2. Sally said, 'When I divide by 4, the only remainders I can get are 1, 2 and 3.'

◧ Investigate this to see if it is true.

☐ Complete this sentence. Circle true or false.

☐ I think the statement is true/false because _____

_____

3. What if you divide a number by 5? What remainders can you get?

◧ Investigate this to find the possible remainders.

☐ Complete this statement:

☐ I think that if you divide by 5 you can get remainders of _____

_____

4. What if you divide a number by 10?

◧ Investigate this to find the possible remainders.

☐ Complete this statement:

☐ I think that if you divide by 10 you can get remainders of

_____

_____

Dear Helper
This activity will help your child to see how remainders work. Encourage your child to start with 10 and divide by 3, then 11 divided by 3, 12 divided by 3 and so on, to see which remainders they can find. Then encourage your child to start with 12 and divide by 4, then 13 divided by 4, 14 divided by 4 (and so on) to see which remainders they can find. When investigating dividing by 5, start with 10 and work up; when investigating dividing by 10, start with 20 and work up.

Name	Date

Number products

2	3	4	5	6	7	8	9

(12) (23) (34) (45) (56) (67) (78) (89)

 See what product you can make by multiplying one of the single-digit numbers above by one of the two-digit numbers.

 Record your written workings in the space below.

 Challenge: See if you can find the largest possible product and then the smallest possible product.

BLOCK E

Dear Helper
This activity aims to revise the skills that your child has been learning this week about using written methods to help solve multiplication questions. Your child has been taught a variety of ways to work out questions and can use any that they would like. Examples of how to work out 24 × 6 are as follows:

a)
×	20	4
6	120	24
= 144

b)
```
  24
×  6
  24  (6 × 4)
 120  (6 × 20)
 144  (6 × 24)
```

c)
```
  24
×  6
 144
   2
```

Name

Date

Decimals equal fractions

■ Look at the containers below.

☐ See if you can spot two containers with equal capacities or masses.

☐ When you spot matching containers, colour them in the same colour.

☐ Beware! Some of the containers do not have a match. Leave these uncoloured.

BLOCK E

Name	Date

Finding equivalent fractions

1									
$\frac{1}{2}$					$\frac{1}{2}$				
$\frac{1}{3}$			$\frac{1}{3}$			$\frac{1}{3}$			
$\frac{1}{4}$		$\frac{1}{4}$		$\frac{1}{4}$			$\frac{1}{4}$		
$\frac{1}{5}$		$\frac{1}{5}$		$\frac{1}{5}$		$\frac{1}{5}$		$\frac{1}{5}$	
$\frac{1}{6}$	$\frac{1}{6}$		$\frac{1}{6}$		$\frac{1}{6}$		$\frac{1}{6}$		$\frac{1}{6}$
$\frac{1}{7}$	$\frac{1}{7}$	$\frac{1}{7}$		$\frac{1}{7}$		$\frac{1}{7}$		$\frac{1}{7}$	$\frac{1}{7}$
$\frac{1}{8}$	$\frac{1}{8}$	$\frac{1}{8}$	$\frac{1}{8}$		$\frac{1}{8}$		$\frac{1}{8}$	$\frac{1}{8}$	$\frac{1}{8}$
$\frac{1}{9}$	$\frac{1}{9}$	$\frac{1}{9}$	$\frac{1}{9}$	$\frac{1}{9}$		$\frac{1}{9}$	$\frac{1}{9}$	$\frac{1}{9}$	$\frac{1}{9}$
$\frac{1}{10}$	$\frac{1}{10}$	$\frac{1}{10}$	$\frac{1}{10}$	$\frac{1}{10}$	$\frac{1}{10}$	$\frac{1}{10}$	$\frac{1}{10}$	$\frac{1}{10}$	$\frac{1}{10}$

◖ Equivalent fractions are two fractions that represent the same part of one whole (for example, $\frac{2}{4}$ is equivalent to $\frac{1}{2}$).

◖ Use the grid to help you write an equivalent fraction for each of these:

$\frac{1}{2}$		$\frac{3}{9}$	
$\frac{1}{4}$		$\frac{4}{10}$	
$\frac{3}{4}$		$\frac{6}{9}$	
1 whole		$\frac{2}{8}$	
$\frac{2}{5}$		$\frac{3}{5}$	
$\frac{2}{3}$		$\frac{8}{10}$	
$\frac{4}{6}$		$\frac{3}{7}$	
$\frac{6}{8}$			

BLOCK E

Dear Helper

This activity helps your child to practise finding equivalent fractions. The fraction chart can be very useful! When your child has finished with this sheet, copy it and cut out the grid. This can be mounted on card and used as a handy reference tool at home or for school.

Name   Date

Ratio and proportion

◼ Ratio and proportion help us to compare amounts.

◼ Complete these statements.

1. There are ⬚ dogs for every ⬚ cats.

2. There are ⬚ squares for every ⬚ triangles.

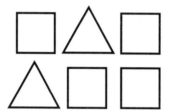

3. In this set there are ⬚ dogs and ⬚ cats.
There are ⬚ dogs for every ⬚ cats.

4. Each day I walk my dog for two hours. How long will I have I walked my dog in total after 5 days? _____

Dear Helper
This activity helps your child to practise finding ratios. Ratio and proportion is a tricky area which many children find difficult. When working with ratios, keep the words and the numbers in the same order. You can also simplify ratios by dividing each side by the same number (for example, the ratio 6:3 is the same as 2:1).

BLOCK E

Puzzles and problems: Objectives grid

The puzzles and problems activities can be used very flexibly to provide children with fun maths tasks to take home. The puzzles and problems are based on work that children will be covering during the year and should test their use and application of mathematics at an appropriate level. Where possible, children should be encouraged to try different approaches to solving these problems and to look for clues and patterns in mathematics.

The grid below lists each activity and identifies links to the different objectives within the Using and applying mathematics strand of the Renewed Framework.

	Solve one-step and two-step problems involving numbers, money or measures, including time; choose and carry out appropriate calculations, using calculator methods where appropriate	Represent a puzzle or problem using number sentences, statements or diagrams; use these to solve the problem; present and interpret the solution in the context of the problem	Suggest a line of enquiry and the strategy needed to follow it; collect, organise and interpret selected information to find answers	Identify and use patterns, relationships and properties of numbers or shapes; investigate a statement involving numbers and test it with examples	Report solutions to puzzles and problems, giving explanations and reasoning orally and in writing, using diagrams and symbols
1 Make a number				✔	
2 Nine-times table trick				✔	
3 Froggie goes a-leaping	✔				
4 Frankie says	✔				
5 Concert tickets	✔				
6 Lucky numbers				✔	
7 Take three ingredients	✔				
8 Picture this				✔	
9 Princess Numberlina				✔	
10 Football attendance			✔		
11 At the sales	✔				
12 Shaun the Shape				✔	
13 Calculator correction			✔		
14 Darts checkout	✔				
15 Pocket money puzzle	✔				
16 Bags of sweets					✔
17 Heavy hamster			✔		
18 Tally Ho!			✔		
19 London to Paris					✔
20 Vegetable weigh-in	✔			✔	
21 Big bottle				✔	
22 Market stall	✔				
23 Marathon times	✔				
24 Sprinting snail	✔				
25 Dance floor	✔				
26 Magic potion	✔				
27 Go-carts	✔				
28 Glen and Glenda				✔	
29 Conkers (1)	✔				
30 Conkers (2)	✔				
31 Swimming pool	✔				
32 Football fans	✔				
33 Phone a friend				✔	
34 Pirate treasure		✔			
35 Marbles	✔				
36 Pocket money					✔

1 Make a number

Alex has four number cards: 5, 8, 2 and 7.

What is the largest number he can make using all four cards?

What is the smallest?

2 Nine-times table trick

Try this neat way to learn the nine-times table.

Put your hands out in front of you, palms upward.

Let's say you want to know what 4×9 is.

From the left, count four fingers in and put that finger down.

The answer is 36. The three fingers to the left of your finger that is down are the 3 (tens) and the six to the right are the 6 (units).

Try it with the other nine-times table facts. It really works!

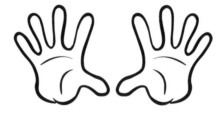

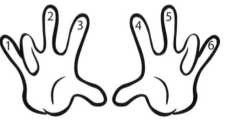

Puzzles and problems

3 Froggie goes a-leaping

Froggie loves leaping over the lily pads.

He leaps seven lily pads in one leap.

He does this six more times, leaping the same distance each time.

How many lily pads has he leapt altogether?

4 Frankie says

Frankie says that the product of his age and his sister's age is 56.

How old could Frankie and his sister be?

There is more than one possible answer!

5 Concert tickets

Tickets to the Locomotives concert cost £8 each.

Bruce has £63.

How many tickets can he buy?

6 Lucky numbers

Jade says the difference between her two lucky numbers under 100 is 17.

What could Jude's lucky numbers be?

Give three suggestions.

1 _____

2 _____

3 _____

7 Take three ingredients

Geena wanted to make an Italian salad.

She bought some mozzarella cheese for £2.18, some tomatoes for 76p and an avocado pear for £1.25.

How much did Geena spend altogether?

8 Picture this

Dane is thinking of a 3D shape.

It has a square base and four other faces which are triangles. What shape is Dane thinking of?

Puzzles and problems

9 Princess Numberlina

Princess Numberlina has lost some numbers from her charm bracelet. Fill in the missing numbers for her.

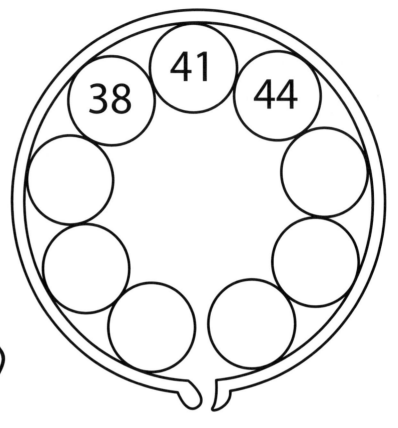

10 Football attendance

Bill went to see his local football team play.

The local newspaper reported that 3200 people were at the game.

This figure was rounded to the nearest 100.

What was the highest number of people that could have been at the game?

_____

What was the lowest number?

_____

PHOTOCOPIABLE ■SCHOLASTIC

11 At the sales

Vicky sees the same bangles in two different shops.

She wants to buy six of them.

Skinflint was selling six for £1, but now they are at half price.

Sillymoney was selling them in packets of two at 30p a packet, but with a 'buy 2, get 1 free' offer.

Where should Vicky buy her six bangles?

How much would she save, compared to buying them from the other shop?

12 Shaun the Shape

Shaun is a regular shape.
Which one is he?

13 Calculator correction

Callum wanted to add 476 and 729 on his new calculator.

However, he typed in 276 + 729 by mistake.

What could Callum do to correct his mistake?

_____

14 Darts checkout

Phil wins a game of darts by scoring treble 20, single 20 then double 20.

What was his total score with his three darts?

15 Pocket money puzzle

Justine's Dad says he will give her £2 pocket money in week one, then double it every week for four weeks if she completes her homework.

How much pocket money will Justine get in total after five weeks?

16 Bags of sweets

Sweet Sue says she has the heaviest bag of sweets because it weighs 2000g.

Sickly Steve says his bag is heavier because it weighs 3kg.

Who has the heavier bag of sweets?

17 Heavy hamster

Hamilton is a heavy hamster!

How much does he weigh?

 g

18 Tally Ho!

Tony made a tally chart to show the wildlife he spotted in the woods near his house in one day.

Animal	Number
Pigeon	### ### ### ### ### ### ### ///
Fox	### /
Rabbit	### ### ### ### //
Badger	///
Deer	###

How many animals did he spot altogether?

Puzzles and problems

19 London to Paris

Hugo First tells his friend Eileen Dover that the distance from London to Paris is 340 metres.

Eileen tells him that part of his answer is wrong.

What should Hugo have said? Why?

_____

_____

_____

20 Vegetable weigh-in

Hussein wanted to find out which was the heaviest of his prize vegetables, so he weighed them. Here are his results:

Onion $\frac{1}{4}$ kg

Marrow 500g

Parsnip 750g

Pumpkin 6kg

Cabbage 1.5kg

Write the list of vegetables in order of weight, heaviest first.

_____

_____

_____

_____

21 Big bottle

Linda bought a big bottle of cherryade from the shop. She said that it contained 100 litres of cherryade.

Sarinda said that was ridiculous and that it held 50 litres of cherryade.

Estimate how much cherryade Linda's bottle really holds.

_____

22 Market stall

Chef Ricardo buys a melon for 88p and 500g of Italian ham at £2.40 per kilo.

How much does he spend altogether?

Puzzles and problems

23 Marathon times

Louis finished running a marathon at 4.30pm.

Hughie ran the same marathon wearing a gorilla suit and finished two hours later.

At what time did Hughie complete the race?

F I N I S H

24 Sprinting snail

Sammy the snail can sprint 75cm in 2 minutes.

If he keeps going at the same speed, how far do you think Sammy can sprint in 4 minutes?

25 Dance floor

The perimeter of a square dance floor is 48m.

What is the length of one side of the dance floor?

_____

26 Magic potion

Merlin has half a litre of magic potion in his flask.

He gives some knights 100ml each until his flask is empty.

How many knights got some magic potion?

Puzzles and problems

27 Go-carts

Jordan wants to hire a petrol go-cart for two hours.

How much will it cost him?

Pedal *GO-KARTS* **£3.50** *per hour*

Petrol *GO-KARTS* **£5.50** *per hour*

28 Glen and Glenda

Glen is 8 years old.

His mum Glenda is 35 years old.

How old was Glenda when Glen was born?

29 Conkers (1)

Sasha has 27 shiny conkers.

She hand out an equal number of conkers to eight of her classmates.

How many conkers does each child get?

30 Conkers (2)

Sasha goes on another conker hunt. This time she finds 19 conkers.

When she shares them out, each classmate gets six conkers and one is left over.

How many classmates receive Sasha's conkers?

Puzzles and problems

31 Swimming pool

Rebecca is doing a sponsored swim to raise money for her school.

Duncan says he will pay her 25p per length.

Rebecca swims seven lengths of the pool.

How much does Duncan pay Rebecca?

32 Football fans

What fraction of these football fans are wearing scarves?

33 Phone a friend

Dave must answer the following question correctly to win the top prize on 'Who wants to win £100?'. He has phoned you for the correct answer!

Which of these is the same as 0.6?

a) 6 out of 12

b) 3 out of 6

c) 6 out of 10

d) 3 out of 9

Which answer should Dave go for?

34 Pirate treasure

Captain Jack is sharing the spoils of his latest daring raid.

He has 208 gold coins to share with three other pirates.

Which of these number sentences is the calculation he needs?

a) 208 × 4

b) 208 – 4

c) 208 + 4

d) 208 ÷ 4

Puzzles and problems

35 Marbles

Nat buys three bags of marbles and pays with a £2 coin.

She gets 20p change.

How much would a single bag of marbles cost?

36 Pocket money

Erin says she gets $\frac{1}{3}$ of £18 every week in pocket money.

Layla says she gets more than that because she receives $\frac{1}{5}$ of £30 each week.

Is Layla correct?

Explain your answer here.

_____

_____

_____

_____

📖 **Homework answers**

Block A

P9 **Times-tables practice** The two numbers that do not fit in the tables are 19 and 23.

P10 **'Less than' snap** No answers.

P11 **Timed challenge** **1** 40; **2** 68; **3** 40; **4** 12; **5** 29; **6** 90; **7** 66; **8** 60; **9** 21; **10** 21.

P12 **Colour by numbers**

6 red	7 blue	8 green	9 yellow	10
16 green	17	45 yellow	19	20
26	27 yellow	28 blue	29	30 red
35 blue	37	38	39	40 green
14 blue	21 blue	12 red	49 blue	50
2	57	58	59	60 red
66 red	32 green	64 green	69	70 blue

1 6 + 12 + 30 + 60 + 66 = 174; **2** 64 − 8 = 56; **3** 4.

P13 **Adding** **1** 100 + 10 = 110; **2** 160 + 12 = 172; **3** 100 + 60 + 8 = 168; **4** 200 + 110 + 14 = 324.

P14 **Multiplication and division practice** 392; 415; 7; 12.

P15 **Counting on** **1** 388; **2** 544; **3** 268; **4** 915; **5** 359; **6** 766.

P16 **Column skills** 494; 251; 188; 676; 716; 922.

P17 **Shopping trip** Answers will vary. One possible answer with maximum items and least change is: Janni buys nine items, cost £2.49, 9p change (3p, 11p, 15p, 26p, 28p, 32p, 34p, 40p, 60p).

P18 **Beat the clock**

23 − 19 = 4	23−21 = 2	36 − 28 = 8
87 - 19 = 68	45 + 21 = 66	70 - 38 = 32
45 + 19 = 64	26 − 21 = 5	37 + 28 = 65
26 − 19 = 7	36 − 21 = 15	56 − 8 = 48
36 − 29 = 7	70 − 31 = 39	25 + 57 = 82
37 + 29 = 66	87 − 28 = 59	29 + 13 = 42
27 + 9 = 36	46 + 18 = 64	

P19 **Subtracting columns** 56; 219; 149; 479; 657; 866.

P20 **The crossing-out challenge** 9; 1 and 99; 76 and 75; 33 and 43, 63 and 73, 69 and 79; 14; 19; 50 and 52; 27.

Block B

P23 **All change!** Answers will vary.

P24 **Missing signs** +; −; ×; −; ÷.

P25 **Next in line** No answers.

P26 **Close enough?** **1** 610 + 290; **2** 20 × 7 or 2 × 10 × 7; **3** 100 − 70; **4** 350 − 100; **5** 1000 + 10; **6** 5 × 10 × 5.

P27 **Nutty nets** No answers.

P28 **Polyfolds** Answers will vary.

P29 **Make it four!** No answers.

P30 **Numbers against the clock** Answers will vary.

P31 **Doubling game** Answers will vary.

P32 **Speed test for 4- and 8-times tables** 16, 32, 8, 20, 28, 4, 12, 36, 40, 24; 24, 64, 8, 40, 56, 16, 80, 48, 32, 72.

P33 **Shape sifting**

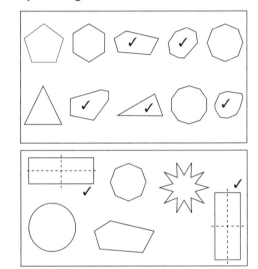

P34 **What makes the box?**
Correct nets for a cube are:

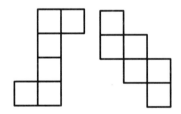

Chocolate box - answers will vary; square-based pyramid.

P35 **Card connect** No answers.

P36 **Sums and products** 6 and 8; 7 and 9; 5 and 5; 3 and 8; 6 and 7; 4 and 9.

P37 **Times-tables investigation** The statement is true.

P38 **Double dice** Answers will vary.

P39 **What a thing to say!** True statements: The sum of two even numbers is always even; The sum of three even numbers is always even; Multiples of 10 always end with a zero; Multiples of 4 will always be even; Odd numbers, when doubled, become even.

📖**SCHOLASTIC**

📖 Homework answers

P40 **Factors 64** 4, 8, 16, 32; **12** 1, 2, 3, 4, 6, 12; **24** 2, 4, 6, 8, 12, 24; **100** 10, 20, 25, 50, 100; **23** 1, 23.

Block C

P43 **Converting lengths** 2cm; 450mm; 0.1m; 6000m; 300cm; 800cm; 0.2km; 40cm; 700mm; 3.5m.

P44 **What will you use?** Fireplace (or hearth rug) – measuring tape or metre rule, m and/or cm; door – measuring tape or metre rule, m and/or cm; finger – ruler, cm or mm; hose – tape measure, m; paw print – ruler, cm or mm; shoe width – ruler or tape measure, cm or mm.

P45 **The shortest distance** 120cm > 8m > 2m > 500cm > 420cm > 345cm > 320cm

P46 **Reading rulers** 7.5cm, 5cm, 8cm, 12.8cm, 6.8cm, 4.5cm, 10.3cm, 7.1cm.

P47 **Favourite days 1** 100; **2** Wednesday; **3** Thursday; **4** 30; **5** Answers will vary; **6** 9.

P48 **Parts of a litre** Vinegar and olive oil (0.75 litre); lemonade and hair mousse (200ml); large pasta sauce and black bean stir-in sauce (800ml); apple juice, milk, orange juice and water (2.5 litres); washing-up liquid, mayonnaise and tomato ketchup (500ml); milk, vegetable oil and orange squash (1.5 litres); wasp sting cream, food colouring and vanilla essence (10ml); hot chilli sauce and soy sauce (0.25 litre); no matches (uncoloured) – nachos sauce, soup, toothpaste and mineral water.

P49 **Bar charts 1** Saturday; **2** Wednesday; **3** Tuesday; **4** Tuesday and Saturday; **5** 135.

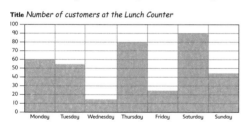

P50 **Reading scales** Answers will vary.

P51 **Carroll families** Answers will vary.

P52 **Workout pictograms** In the top pictogram, show 20 children by drawing four face symbols on the line '4 hours or more'.

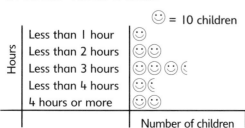

P53 **Battle of the bands**

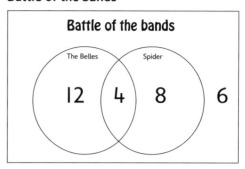

P54 **Music survey 1** Rock; **2** Country; **3** 4; **4** 22; **5** 58.

Block D

P57 **Money, money, money! 1** 20 weeks; **2** £7.20; **3** £2.03; **4** 4 bars.

P58 **Time snap** No answers.

P59 **Estimating and measuring mass** Answers will vary.

P60 **Shapes and coordinates** Answers will vary.

P61 **Talk time** Answers will vary.

P62 **Bright white** Answers will vary.

P63 **Following directions** Answers will vary.

P64 **Calculating answers** $3 \times 8 = 24$; $4 \times 7 = 28$; $6 \times 5 = 30$; $5 \times 9 = 45$; $7 \times 9 = 63$; $8 \times 7 = 56$; $30 \div 6 = 5$; $64 \div 8 = 8$; $24 \div 3 = 8$; $45 \div 9 = 5$; $12 \div 2 = 6$; $50 \div 10 = 5$.

×	20	6	
3	60	18	= 78

×	30	5	
6	180	30	= 210

×	40	7	
4	160	28	= 188

×	50	8	
5	250	40	= 290

×	60	9	
2	120	18	= 138

×	70	3	
7	490	21	= 511

×	80	4	
8	640	32	= 672

×	90	1	
9	810	9	= 819

P65 Angle grinding

4	1	7	5
3	8	6	2

Right angle would fit after angle labelled 3; half a right angle fits after angle labelled 1; half of 360° fits after angle labelled 6.

P66 Estimating and measuring capacity Answers will vary

P67 Trans-Air challenge 1 1 hour 35 minutes; **2** Yes; **3** No; **4** Thursday; **5** 5 minutes; **6** 3 hours 15 minutes (or 3¼ hours); **7** 14.10.

P68 Money columns £13.56 + £8.76 = £22.32
£13.56 + £6.78 = £20.34
£13.56 + £3.14 = £16.70
£13.56 + £2.99 = £16.55
£13.56 + £8.12 = £21.68
£8.76 + £6.78 = £15.54
£8.76 + £3.14 = £11.90
£8.76 + £2.99 = £11.75
£8.76 + £8.12 = £16.88
£6.78 + £3.14 = £9.92
£6.78 + £2.99 = £9.77
£6.78 + £8.12 = £14.90
£3.14 + £2.99 = £6.13
£3.14 + £8.12 = £11.26
£2.99 + £8.12 = £11.11

Block E

P71 Times-tables challenge Answers will vary.

P72 Fraction shapes $^2/_4$ or $^1/_2$; $^1/_3$; $^2/_6$ or $^1/_3$; $^3/_6$ or $^1/_2$; $^2/_{10}$ or $^1/_5$.

P73 Range of numbers Answers will vary.

P74 Focus on fractions Answers will vary.

P75 Multiple magic 6; 15; 90; 60; 12, 24, 36, 48; 52, 56, 60, 64, 68, 72, 76; 60; 15; 90.

P76 Higher or lower? Less than $^1/_2$: $^1/_3$, $^1/_4$, $^1/_5$, $^1/_{10}$, $^3/_8$, 0.01, 0.1, 0.25.
More than $^1/_2$: $^2/_3$, $^3/_4$, $^7/_8$, $^7/_{10}$, $^9/_{10}$, $^4/_5$, 0.6, 1.25, 2.5, 10.1.

P77 Fraction pelmanism No answers.

P78 Equivalence snap No answers.

P79 Dividing codes Divisible by 2 and 3: 6, 12, 18, 24, 30, 36, 60, 72, 78, 90.
Divisible by 2 and 5: 20, 30, 40, 60, 70, 80, 90, 100, 160.
Divisible by 3 and 4: 12, 24, 36, 60, 72.
Divisible by 4 and 5: 20, 40, 60, 80, 100, 160.
Divisible by 2, 3, 4 and 5: 60 (and multiples thereof).

P80 Fractions and decimals $^1/_2$ = 0.5, $^1/_4$ = 0.25, $^1/_{10}$ = 0.1, $^1/_{100}$ = 0.01, $^7/_{14}$ = 0.5, $^2/_8$ = 0.25, $^3/_{10}$ = 0.3, $^{63}/_{100}$ = 0.63, $^6/_{12}$ = 0.5, $^4/_{16}$ = 0.25, $^9/_{10}$ = 0.9, $^{27}/_{100}$ = 0.27.

P81 Making one

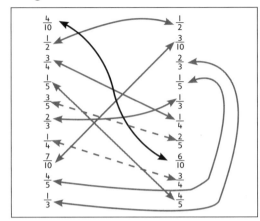

1 $^1/_6$; **2** $^4/_7$; **3** $^3/_8$; **4** $^8/_9$.

P82 Fractions of shapes Answers will vary.

P83 Remaining remainders 1 12 months, £3 change; **2** 4 books, £4 left; **3** 18 packs, with one glue left over; **4** 6 piles, 6 extra chairs; **5** 6 packs of 4, 1 left; **6** £2.60 each, no money left over.

**P84 Are you certain?
1** True; **2** True; **3** Possible remainders are 1, 2, 3 and 4; **4** Possible remainders are 1, 2, 3, 4, 5, 6, 7, 8 and 9.

P85 Number products Largest possible product 801; smallest possible product 24.

P86 Decimals equal fractions Mineral water and olive oil (7.5 litres); vinegar, large pasta sauce and fruit smoothie (0.75 litres); soy sauce and brown sauce (0.25 pints); herbs and chilli powder (2.5g); milk and orange juice (2.5 pints); toothpaste and wasp sting cream (3.5 oz); mayonnaise and black bean stir-in sauce (250g); lip balm and lens cleaner (2.25g).

P87 Finding equivalent fractions (Of the fractions illustrated in the grid): $^1/_2$ = $^2/_4$ = $^3/_6$ = $^4/_8$ = $^5/_{10}$; $^1/_4$ = $^2/_8$; $^3/_4$ = $^6/_8$; 1 whole = $^2/_2$ = $^3/_3$ = $^4/_4$ = $^5/_5$ = $^6/_6$ = $^7/_7$ = $^8/_8$ = $^9/_9$ = $^{10}/_{10}$; $^2/_5$ = $^4/_{10}$; $^2/_3$ = $^4/_6$ = $^6/_9$; $^4/_6$ = $^2/_3$; $^6/_8$ = $^3/_4$; $^3/_9$ = $^1/_3$ = $^2/_6$; $^4/_{10}$ = $^2/_5$; $^6/_9$ = $^2/_3$ = $^4/_6$; $^2/_8$ = $^1/_4$; $^3/_5$ = $^6/_{10}$; $^8/_{10}$ = $^4/_5$; $^3/_7$ is not equivalent to any other fraction shown on the grid.

P88 Ratio and proportion 2 dogs for every 4 cats (or 1 dog for every 2 cats); 4 squares for every 2 triangles (or 2 squares for every 1 triangle); 6 dogs for every 2 cats (or 3 dogs for every 1 cat); 10 hours.

Puzzles and problems answers

1 **Make a number** 8752; 2578

2 **Nine-times table trick** No answer required.

3 **Froggie goes a-leaping** 49

4 **Frankie says** 7 and 8 years old (other answers could include 4 and 14 years; 2 and 28 years; 1 and 56 years).

5 **Concert tickets** 7 tickets

6 **Lucky numbers** Answers will vary. Three possibilities are: 99 and 82, 50 and 33, 20 and 3.

7 **Take three ingredients** £4.19

8 **Picture this** A square-based pyramid

9 **Princess Numberlina** 29, 32, 35, 47, 50, 53

10 **Football attendance** 3249; 3150

11 **At the sales** Skinflint; save 10p

12 **Shaun the Shape** The equilateral triangle

13 **Calculator correction** Add 200

14 **Darts checkout** 120

15 **Pocket money puzzle** £62

16 **Bags of sweets** Sickly Steve

17 **Heavy hamster** 250g

18 **Tally Ho!** 74

19 **London to Paris** 340 kilometres

20 **Vegetable weigh-in** Pumpkin, cabbage, parsnip, marrow, onion

21 **Big bottle** 1–2 litres

22 **Market stall** £2.08

23 **Marathon times** 6.30pm

24 **Sprinting snail** 150cm or 1.5m

25 **Dance floor** 12m

26 **Magic potion** 5 knights

27 **Go-carts** £11

28 **Glen and Glenda** 27 years old

29 **Conkers (1)** 3 conkers

30 **Conkers (2)** 3 classmates

31 **Swimming pool** £1.75

32 **Football fans** $9/12$ or ¾

33 **Phone a friend** (c) 6 out of 10

34 **Pirate treasure** (d) 208 ÷ 4

35 **Marbles** 60p

36 **Pocket money** No, they both get the same amount ($1/3 \times £18 = £6$; $1/5 \times £30 = £6$).

SCHOLASTIC

Also available in this series:

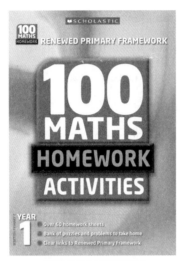

ISBN 978-1407-10216-0

ISBN 978-1407-10217-7

ISBN 978-1407-10218-4

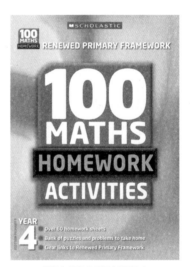

ISBN 978-1407-10219-1

ISBN 978-1407-10220-7

ISBN 978-1407-10221-4

To find out more, call: 0845 603 9091
or visit our website www.scholastic.co.uk